MW01502533

URBAN GURU

PITTSBURGH

*Written by Amy Campbell, Bridget Daley,
Matt Hamman, and Jen Vella*

*Layout and Edits by Amy Campbell, Bridget Daley,
Matt Hamman, and Jen Vella*

Final Edits by Amy Campbell

ISBN # 978-1-4274-0324-7
www.collegeprowler.com/urbanguru

Last updated: 12/10/08

College Prowler®
5001 Baum Blvd.
Suite 750
Pittsburgh, PA 15213

Phone: 1-800-290-2682
Fax: 1-800-772-4972
urbanguru@collegeprowler.com
www.collegeprowler.com/urbanguru

Welcome to Urban Guru®

Moving to a new city for college or a job is stressful, and it takes time to adjust, but getting comfortable is key to making the most of your new surroundings.

I learned this first-hand when I traveled more than 2500 miles from my hometown to attend college. The first six months were awesome. My new city was an exciting new place, and I was eager to explore it. But then I started to stick to the same old stuff instead of continuing to try new things, and after a while those exciting things got a little boring and repetitive.

I was anxious to get out of my comfort zone, so I went to a local bookstore and purchased two guides to the city. I learned about a couple of cool new places, but since these books weren't written with college students, recent graduates, or young professionals in mind, the author's perspective didn't match what I was looking for—I needed real insider information.

To get the inside scoop, I sought out individuals who really knew the area and started peppering them with questions: What are the best restaurants? What events do I have to check out? What are the up-and-coming neighborhoods? I kept asking as many different people as I could find, and now I know the lay of the land as if I had grown up here my whole life. My success was built on finding passionate people to tell me about all their favorite things and talking to as many varied sources as possible.

This is how we built our original College Prowler series, and it's the same approach we took for the new Urban Guru series. We sought out as many sources as possible, and we talked to locals who were eager to tell their insider secrets.

As always, we're dying to hear how this guide helped you or how you think it can be improved. Any and all feedback is always welcomed. Our goal is to create the most helpful guides possible to take the stress and discomfort out of moving to a new city. We hope that this guide helps you hit the ground running faster than you would have on your own.

Luke Skurman, CEO and co-founder
lukeskurman@collegeprowler.com

Introduction to Pittsburgh

After receiving the title of America's Most Livable City for the second time, the people of Pittsburgh can look around and certainly be proud of this once-booming steel mill town. Pittsburgh today is home to some of the best universities in the country, world-class doctors and hospitals, internationally successful companies, trendy shopping districts, rich cultural attractions, a lively nightlife, and most notably—well, at least, to the diehard fans—some of the best professional sports teams in the country.

With a low cost of living and a beautiful cityscape, Pittsburgh makes for an ideal city that is so much more than developments and chain stores. Often called the "City of Bridges" thanks to the almost 450 bridges that dot the hills and riversides, Pittsburgh has found a way to successfully bridge the gap between big-city excitement and small-town charm. A visit to the Strip District will fill your stomach and fridge with some of the freshest ingredients around. In one trip down East Carson Street in the South Side, you will pass more bars and restaurants than you can count. A tour of Oakland could take you back to the days of the dinosaurs at the Carnegie Museum of Natural History, to a robotics institute at Carnegie Mellon University, or to the forefront of medical advancements at the University of Pittsburgh Medical Center. And that's just three of the 90 individual neighborhoods making up the City of Pittsburgh.

Offering an insider take from the locals' perspective, the *Urban Guru* guide to Pittsburgh aims to give an in-depth look at life in the Steel City—both the good and the bad. From the best restaurants and bars to which neighborhoods to live in, this guide tells it how the locals see it on nearly every aspect of life. Whatever your reason for coming to the 'Burgh, the city offers more than enough reasons to stay. Welcome to Pittsburgh! You just might surprise yourself and fall in love with all this city has to offer.

Table of Contents

Pittsburgh By Numbers

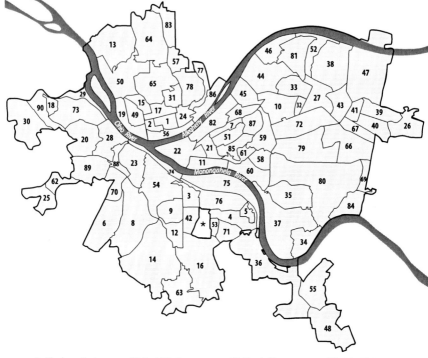

1. Allegheny Center
2. Allegheny West
3. Allentown
4. Arlington
5. Arlington Heights
6. Banksville
7. Bedford Dwellings
8. Beechview
9. Beltzhoover
10. Bloomfield
11. Bluff (aka Uptown)
12. Bon Air
13. Brighton Heights
14. Brookline
15. California-Kirkbride
16. Carrick
17. Central Northside
18. Chartiers
19. Chateau
20. Crafton Heights
21. Crawford-Roberts
22. Downtown
    (aka Central Business
    District, The Golden
    Triangle)
23. Duquesne Heights

24. East Allegheny
25. East Carnegie
26. East Hills
27. East Liberty
28. Elliot
29. Esplen
30. Fairywood
31. Fineview
32. Friendship
33. Garfield
34. Glen Hazel
35. Greenfield
36. Hays
37. Hazelwood
38. Highland Park
39. Homewood North
40. Homewood South
41. Homewood West
42. Knoxville
43. Larimer
44. Central Lawrenceville
45. Lower Lawrenceville
46. Upper Lawrenceville
47. Lincoln-Lemington-
    Belmar

48. Lincoln Place
49. Manchester
50. Marshall-Shadeland
    (aka Brightwood)
51. Middle Hill District
52. Morningside
53. Mount Oliver
54. Mount Washington
55. New Homestead
56. North Shore
57. Northview Heights
58. Central Oakland
59. North Oakland
60. South Oakland
61. West Oakland
62. Oakwood
63. Overbrook
64. Perry North
    (aka Observatory Hill)
65. Perry South
    (aka Perry Hilltop)
66. Point Breeze
67. Point Breeze North
68. Polish Hill
69. Regent Square
70. Ridgemont

71. Saint Clair
72. Shadyside
73. Sheraden
74. Southshore
75. South Side Flats
76. South Side Slopes
77. Spring Garden
78. Spring Hill-City View
79. Squirrel Hill North
80. Squirrel Hill South
81. Stanton Heights
82. Strip District
83. Summer Hill
84. Swisshelm Park
85. Terrace Village
86. Troy Hill
87. Upper Hill District
88. West End
89. Westwood
90. Windgap

* The Borough of
Mt. Oliver is not an
official part of the city.

Pittsburgh at a Glance

The Lowdown On...
Facts & Figures

Region:
Southwestern Pennsylvania

County:
Allegheny County

Population:
City: 311,218
Metro Area: 2,370,776
Density: 6,028 per sq. mi.

Founded:
November 25, 1758

Size:
58.3 square miles

Elevation:
1,223 feet

Area Codes:
412, 724, 878

Zip Codes:
15201–15235

→

Population by Gender:
Female: 52%
Male: 48%

Population by Age:
Under 18: 20%
20–34: 25%
35–64: 39%
Over 65: 16%

Birth Rate:
10.5 per 1,000

Death Rate:
11.9 per 1,000

Median Age:
35.5 (National average: 35.3)

Enrolled in College or Graduate School:
13%

Bachelor's Degree or Higher:
26%

Population Growth:
-1% since 1990

Weather

Average Temperature:
Fall: 44°F–62°F
Winter: 23°F–38°F
Spring: 39°F–60°F
Summer: 60°F–81°F

Average Precipitation:
Fall: 2.83 in.
Winter: 2.78 in.
Spring: 3.33 in.
Summer: 3.82 in.

City Web Sites
www.pittsburgh.net
www.city.pittsburgh.pa.us
www.visitpittsburgh.com
www.pittsburgh.com

www.collegeprowler.com/urbanguru

Points of Interest:

Andy Warhol Museum
North Shore

August Wilson Center for African American Culture
Cultural District, Downtown

Carnegie Museums of Art and Natural History
Oakland

Carnegie Science Center
North Shore

Cathedral of Learning and Nationality Rooms
University of Pittsburgh, Oakland

Children's Museum of Pittsburgh
North Side

Duquesne & Monongahela Inclines
Mt. Washington/Station Square

Frick Art & Historical Center
Point Breeze

Frick Park
Point Breeze/Squirrel Hill

The Great Allegheny Passage
McKeesport

Heinz Field
North Shore

Heinz History Center
Strip District

Kennywood Park
West Mifflin

The Mattress Factory
North Side

Mellon Arena
Downtown

The National Aviary
North Side

Phipps Conservatory and Botanical Gardens
Schenley Park, Oakland

Pittsburgh Zoo & PPG Aquarium
Highland Park

PNC Park
North Shore

Point State Park
Downtown

PPG Place
Downtown

Sandcastle Waterpark
Homestead

SouthSide Works
South Side

Station Square and the Gateway Clipper
Southern end of the Smithfield Street Bridge

The Waterfront
Homestead/Munhall

U.S. Steel Tower
Downtown

Did You Know?

Fun Facts About Pittsburgh

- In an attempt to standardize city names, **"Pittsburgh" was officially changed to "Pittsburg" in 1891**. Many locals refused to acknowledge the new spelling, however, and the name was officially changed back in 1911.

- Pittsburgh was chosen as **America's Most Livable City** by *Places Rated Almanac* in 2007. Of the 379 metro areas surveyed, Pittsburgh topped the list based on cost of living, transportation, jobs, education, climate, crime, health care, recreation, and cultural ambience.

- *Mister Rogers' Neighborhood* **was produced at the community-sponsored WQED studio** in Oakland. It is the longest-running series on PBS.

- In 1979, Carnegie Mellon University established **the first robotics institute to conduct basic and applied research** in robotics technologies relevant to industrial and everyday tasks. It was the first university in the world to offer a Ph.D. in robotics, and its Robotics Institute is still one of the leading places to study robotics in the world.

Pittsburgh Nicknames

The Steel City

The Iron City

The 'Burgh

The City of Bridges

The City of Champions (mostly for the Steelers and the Pirates in the '70s)

Famous People from the Pittsburgh Area

Christina Aguilera, Kurt Angle, Jeff Goldblum, Ken Griffey and Ken Griffey Jr., Michael Keaton, Dennis Miller, Joe Montana, Demi Moore, Ming-Na, Joe Namath, Trent Reznor, George Romero, Gertrude Stein, Jimmy Stewart, Honus Wagner, Andy Warhol

Neighborhoods

The Lowdown On...
Neighborhoods

City Neighborhoods

In the diverse and eclectic city of Pittsburgh, there are 90 individual and culturally rich neighborhoods.

City Taxes

Property taxes in Allegheny County are determined by property value and three local millage rates—county, municipal, and school district. Those living in the City of Pittsburgh pay .469% of their home value to the county, 1.08 to the city, and 1.392% to the school district

Young and Hip Neighborhoods:

Bloomfield
Downtown Pittsburgh
Highland Park
Lawrenceville
Mt. Washington
North Side
Oakland
Point Breeze
Shadyside
South Side
Squirrel Hill
Strip District

Bloomfield
Pittsburgh's Little Italy

Located three miles from Downtown,
Bloomfield is a culturally diverse
neighborhood in Pittsburgh.
Renowned as Pittsburgh's Little Italy,
Bloomfield offers a colorful mix of restaurants and shops.

Neighborhood Web Site

www.shoppingbloomfield.com/ overview

Average Listing Price

$208,156

Average Monthly Rent

$575–$900 for two bedrooms

Best Place to Shop

Along Liberty Avenue

Best Eats

Tessaro's for burgers
Café Roma

Best Cafés or Coffee Shops

Crazy Mocha

Popular Salon

Salon Bella Mia

Neighborhood Festivals/Fairs

Little Italy Days (September)

Nearest Hospital

Children's Hospital
West Penn Hospital

Hidden Treasures

The Evaline Street Halloween
Party, a longtime Bloomfield
tradition, was chosen by
SPIN magazine as one of the
coolest Halloween events in
the country.

"**Bloomfield is an up-and-coming neighborhood** with a lot of new bars and young professionals around town."

Downtown Pittsburgh
Cultural District

With breathtaking views and cultural attractions, Downtown Pittsburgh is also home to more than 2,000 residents seeking the convenience of downtown living.

Neighborhood Web Site

www.downtownpittsburgh.com

Average Listing Price

$371,870

Average Monthly Rent

$900–$2,400 for two bedrooms

Best Place to Shop

Along Liberty Avenue

Best Eats

Capital Grille

Seviche

Six Penn Kitchen

Best Cafés or Coffee Shops

Nicholas Coffee

Neighborhood Gym

Gold's Gym

Popular Salons

Brett James Salon

Salon Christine

Spa Uptown

Neighborhood Festivals/Fairs

Three Rivers Arts Festival (June)

Light-Up Night (November)

First Night (December 31)

Nearest Hospital

UPMC Mercy

Hidden Treasures

Each year at Light-Up Night, the Rink at PPG Place downtown opens to the public for ice skating and becomes the perfect place to host holiday movie-worthy memories.

Highland Park
Home of the Zoo

Located among the beautiful landscape and hills of the neighborhood's namesake park, Highland Park is a perfect example of residential living near the city center.

Neighborhood Web Site

www.highlandpark.pgh.pa.us

Average Listing Price

$241,065

Average Monthly Rent

$650–$950 for two bedrooms

Best Places to Shop

Along North Highland Avenue

Best Eats

Joseph Tambellini Restaurant

Reynold's on Bryant Restaurant

Best Cafés or Coffee Shops

Enrico's Tazza D'Oro

Neighborhood Festivals/Fairs

Highland Fling (May)

Nearest Hospital

West Penn Hospital

Hidden Treasures

Take a hands-on cooking class from Food Glorious Food (*www.foodgloriousfoodonline.com*).

"I love living in Highland Park. You are a short bus ride to Downtown and the universities. Plus, there is **a beautiful park within walking distance**."

Lawrenceville
16:62 Design Zone

One of Pittsburgh's largest and oldest neighborhoods, Lawrenceville has seen a recent influx of artists, musicians, and young professionals to the up-and-coming neighborhood.

Neighborhood Web Site

lawrenceville-pgh.com

Average Listing Price

Lower Lawrenceville – $248,143

Central Lawrenceville – $135,911

Average Monthly Rent

$550–$950 for two bedrooms

Best Place to Shop

Along Butler Street

Best Eats

Piccolo Forno

Tram's Kitchen

Best Cafés or Coffee Shops

Coca Café

> "**Lawrenceville is very up-and-coming** for young people. Very hip."

Neighborhood Festivals/Fairs

Arsenal Park Independence Day Celebration (Saturday after July 4)

Art All Night (Last Saturday in April)

Lawrenceville Hospitality House Tour (October)

Nearest Hospital

Children's Hospital

West Penn Hospital

Hidden Treasures

Paint your own pottery at Kiln-N-Time

Roberto Clemente Museum

Mt. Washington
Best Views of the City

USA Weekend magazine named the view from Mt. Washington one of the top 10 most beautiful in the country. The neighborhood combines affordably priced homes with a prime location—all just an incline ride from Station Square.

Neighborhood Web Site

www.mwcdc.org

Average Listing Price

$98,733

Average Monthly Rent

$650–$1,200 for two bedrooms

Best Eats with a View

LeMont

Monterey Bay

Tin Angel

Best Cafés or Coffee Shops

Café Cravings

Best Place to Take a Skyline Picture

Grandview Avenue

Nearest Hospitals

UPMC Mercy

Hidden Treasures

Farmers' market, Tuesdays at St. Mary of the Mount Church

Top Honors

MSN.com ranked Pittsburgh's Duquesne Incline as one of the top romantic spots in the country, both for the ride and for the spectacular views from the top of Mt. Washington

"Mt. Washington is the perfect little area to reside in because it has absolutely everything you need. And, of course, **you can't forget about the view**."

North Side
The Heart of Pittsburgh Sports and Museums

Home to the Mexican War Streets, Heinz Field, PNC Park, Children's Museum of Pittsburgh, Carnegie Science Center, Andy Warhol Museum, and The Mattress Factory, the North Side collectively describes the 18 neighborhoods that wrap around the northern banks of the Allegheny and Ohio rivers and climb up the adjacent hillsides.

Neighborhood Web Site

www.pittsburghnorthside.com

Average Listing Price

Central North Side – $199,723

Average Monthly Rent

$650–$1,700 for two bedrooms

Best Eats

Atria's Restaurant

New Moon Fusion Restaurant

Penn Brewery Restaurant

Best Cafés or Coffee Shops

Beleza Community Coffeeshop

Buon Giorno Café

The Café 'n' Creamery

Top Art Museums

The Andy Warhol Museum

The Mattress Factory

Neighborhood Festivals/Fairs

Oktoberfest at Penn Brewery (September)

Nearest Hospital

Allegheny General Hospital

Hidden Treasures

Fridays at the Warhol

House tours of the Mexican War Streets

Making your own T-shirts at Artists Image Resource

Summertime jazz concerts in Riverview Park in the Observatory Hill neighborhood

Oakland
Academic, Cultural, and Health Care Center

Don't be fooled—Oakland isn't just for college students. Oakland is home to art museums, history centers, Phipps Conservatory, eclectic restaurants, and swanky coffee shops.

"Oakland is one of the main young and hip neighborhoods. **It's a good location** for bars and such."

Neighborhood Web Site

www.onlyinoakland.org

Average Listing Price

North Oakland – $726,247
West Oakland – $134,900
South Oakland – $100,157

Average Monthly Rent

$700–$1,300 for two bedrooms

Best Places to Shop

Along Forbes Avenue and South Craig Street

Best Eats

Indian Garden
Mad Mex

Best Cafés or Coffee Shops

Kiva Han
Crazy Mocha

Neighborhood Festivals/Fairs

Greek Food Festival at St. Nicholas Greek Orthodox Cathedral (May)

Nearest Hospitals

In the heart of Oakland are six of UPMC's hospitals.

Hidden Treasures

Rotating exhibits at Phipps Conservatory and Botanical Gardens

Point Breeze
Rich History Meets Stately Charm

Once home to famous Pittsburghers like Heinz, Frick, and Carnegie, Point Breeze still reflects the beauty of gracious homes, wrought-iron fences, and cul-de-sacs.

Neighborhood Web Site

outside.in/Point_Breeze_Pittsburgh_PA

Average Listing Price

$372,358

Average Monthly Rent

$700–$1,000

Best Eats

Pino's Mercato

Best Cafés or Coffee Shops

Point Brugge Café

Neighborhood Festivals/Fairs

First Fridays at Frick Park (summer)

Nearest Hospital

West Penn Hospital

Literary Fame

Annie Dillard set her memoir in Point Breeze

John Edgar Wideman uses Westinghouse Park as a setting for one of his fictional books

Hidden Treasures

Frick Art & Historical Center

Mellon Park

Westinghouse Park

"Point Breeze is one of the smaller, lesser-known **neighborhoods that is a cool place** to live."

Shadyside
The Georgetown of Pittsburgh

The neighborhood for the young and hip in the city, Shadyside offers an endless variety of restaurants, bars, boutiques, and coffee shops.

> "Shadyside has a good atmosphere for young professionals. **It has that neighborhood feel** to it."

Neighborhood Web Site
www.shadysideshops.com

Average Listing Price
$387,188

Average Monthly Rent
$800–$2,000

Best Places to Shop
Along Walnut Street or Ellsworth Avenue

Best Eats
Girasole

Soba

Best Cafés or Coffee Shops
Jitters Café

Oh Yeah! Ice Cream & Coffee

Neighborhood Gyms
Fitness Factory

X Shadyside Health & Fitness

Best Salon
Capristo Salon

Neighborhood Festivals/Fairs
Shadyside Arts Festival (September)

Jam on Walnut (summer)

Nearest Hospitals
Hillman Cancer Center

UPMC Shadyside

Hidden Treasures
Prantl's Bakery

South Side
The Great Pittsburgh Main Street

The options for restaurants, bars, shops, and music venues on East Carson Street are seemingly endless. Made up of the Flats and Slopes, the South Side is a popular neighborhood for longtime residents, college students, and professionals alike.

Neighborhood Web Site

www.southsidepgh.com

Average Listing Price

South Side Flats – $298,061
South Side Slopes – $187,186

Average Monthly Rent

$700–$1,400

Best Places to Shop

Along East Carson Street and in the SouthSide Works

Best Eats

Dish Osteria
Gypsy Café
Ibiza Tapas & Wine Bar
Nakama Japanese Steakhouse and Sushi Bar

Best Cafés or Coffee Shops

The Beehive

Neighborhood Gyms

East Carson Fitness
South Side Athletic Club

Popular Salons

deStefino Southside
Uzori

Nearest Hospital

UPMC Mercy

Hidden Treasures:

Morning Glory Inn

"**South Side is a very trendy place to live.** The are lots of bars, shops, and restaurants."

Squirrel Hill
Pittsburgh Most Diverse Neighborhood

An upscale, family-friendly neighborhood in Pittsburgh, Squirrel Hill is known for its variety of ethnic restaurants, diverse shops, and Jewish community, which includes 20 synagogues.

Neighborhood Web Sites

www.shuc.org
www.squirrelhill.com

Average Listing Price

Squirrel Hill North – $563,124
Squirrel Hill South – $261,835

Average Monthly Rent

$725–$1,600

Best Places to Shop

Along Murray and Forbes avenues

Best Eats

Aladdin's Eatery
Bangkok Balcony
Gullifty's Restaurant
Mineo's Pizza House
Sweet Basil/La Filipiniana

Best Cafés or Coffee Shops

Coffee Tree Roasters
The 61C Café

Neighborhood Parks

Frick Park
Schenley Park

Nearest Hospital

UPMC Shadyside

Hidden Treasures

East End Chocolate Stout cupcakes from Dozen
$3 records at Jerry's Records
Walking trails at Frick Park

"**Squirrel Hill is a bit more quiet and residential**, but there's still plenty going on."

Strip District
Pittsburgh's Historic Market District

Combining a variety of fresh markets, ethnic grocers, quality restaurants, unique cafés, and bustling nightlife, the Strip District is one of Pittsburgh's liveliest neighborhoods.

Neighborhood Web Site

www.neighborsinthestrip.com

Average Listing Price

$593,760

Average Monthly Rent

$1,100–$1,500

Best Places to Shop

Along Penn Avenue

The Strip is the go-to place for fresh food, imported delights, and some of the finest ingredients you can find in the 'Burgh—make a Sunday morning out of it.

Best Eats

Eleven

Kaya

Lidia's Pittsburgh

Wholey's Fish Market

Best Cafés or Coffee Shops

21st Street Coffee and Tea

La Prima Espresso Roastery

Leaf & Bean

For the Sweet Tooth

Enrico Biscotti Company

Klavon's Authentic Ice Cream Parlor

Mon Aimee Chocolat

Nearest Hospital

UPMC Mercy

Hidden Treasures

First Friday Dinners every month at Enrico Biscotti

Free brown bag opera concerts hosted by the Pittsburgh Opera Center Saturdays in the Strip

Locals Speak Out On...
Neighborhoods

"**Shadyside is a very popular place for the young crowds who make a bit more money. It is pricey but worth it.**"

Q "Shadyside, Squirrel Hill, Mt. Washington, and the South Side are the most young and hip neighborhoods, in my opinion. Of those, **Shadyside and Squirrel Hill would be my picks as places to live** simply because they are a little safer than the other two and offer plenty of shops, bars, restaurants, and other neighborhood amenities."

Q "**You can find a decent place to live** in Oakland, Shadyside, or Highland Park."

Q "**Shadyside and Squirrel Hill have everything a young professional could want**—nice local restaurants, gyms and workout facilities, and locations close to Downtown."

Q "I would say Friendship has nice, old, **beautiful houses that are affordable**."

Q "The young areas in Pittsburgh are the South Side and Shadyside. They have the easiest access to local bars and restaurants, so **they have the highest population of 20-somethings**."

Q "My favorite neighborhood in Pittsburgh is definitely Squirrel Hill. **It is a vibrant community with a few beautiful residential areas and a business district** filled with a lot of fun and unique shops. There is also a wide variety of restaurants, offering many different types of food, everything from Japanese to Lebanese to Thai to Italian."

Q "**The South Side boasts Pittsburgh's most active nightlife spots on East Carson Street.** You can find an array of bars, clubs, restaurants, shops, and live music venues, all of which can suit almost any taste. Also, development of and in this area is booming."

Q "Lawrenceville/Bloomfield is arguably **the most young and hip area.**"

Q "Shadyside has its own nightlife, so you don't have to travel far for a good time. Rent could be pretty cheap to average—it all depends on what streets and how close they are to certain things. Buying, however, can be a little tricky. **You can find townhouses and small homes in the area for a decent price, but the taxes are killer.**"

Q "**There are some transitional neighborhoods on the North Side**—nice during the day, but not at night."

Q "North Oakland is the neighboring region to Shadyside. It's not as nice and has fewer attractions, but **the cost of living is lower.** You can stay in really nice places anywhere from $550 to $950 a month, depending on how many bedrooms and baths."

Q "**Greenfield is cheaper than Squirrel Hill** and a bit more seedy and run down, but it's still a decent place to live on a budget."

Q "**We moved to an up-and-coming neighborhood when we came to Pittsburgh.** There is so much renovation right now it's crazy! I think the home prices are very reasonable at this time because the area is still changing."

Q "The best neighborhoods are Shadyside and the South Side. In both cases, **there is a tremendous amount of things to do within walking distance** and tons of young people looking to have fun. Also, they are reasonable places to live."

Q "**Pittsburgh has a lot of great, hip neighborhoods**, namely Shadyside, the South Side, Point Breeze, and Squirrel Hill."

Q "**The South Side and Oakland seem to be the most youthful neighborhoods** since many of their inhabitants are college students."

Q "The South Side is closest to the city and has the best bars, but **watch out for random vandalism from drunken bar goers**. If you like to relax, the best place to live is Shadyside. It's laid-back, gay, and friendly!"

Q Shadyside and Squirrel Hill have **everything a young professional could want**—nice local restaurants, gyms/workout facilities, and a location close to Downtown. Shadyside also has its own nightlife, so you don't have to travel far for a good time."

Q "I would live in Bloomfield or Friendship. **There are many inexpensive bars and restaurants in Bloomfield**, and you are close to Shadyside, Lawrenceville, and Downtown."

Q "There are housing options for most price ranges. **The dollar does not go as far in Shadyside** as it does in some other areas, but I think it's worth it."

Q "Lawrenceville is the most interesting developing neighborhood. Local business owners have been very energetic in encouraging design-related stores. It is definitely an interesting place to go, and it's more adult than the South Side. **It's a wonderful example of urban development from the ground up**."

Q "South Side is a little loud, but it's vibrant and exciting. **Lawrenceville is up-and-coming**, so there are all sorts of DIY restaurants, bars, and art houses popping up."

Lifestyles

The Lowdown On...
Lifestyles

Median Home Price:

Pittsburgh	$127,700
National Average	$220,800

Cost of Living:

16.4 percent lower than the national average

Households:

Single householder:	39.4%
Married couples:	31.2%
Families with children:	21.9%

Housing Resources:

www.craigslist.org
www.pittsburghmoves.com
www.rentalguidepittsburgh.com
www.trulia.com

Top Family-Friendly Destinations in the City:

Carnegie Museums
Carnegie Science Center
Children's Museum of Pittsburgh
Kennywood Park
Pittsburgh Zoo & PPG Aquarium

→

Animal Shelters:

Animal Friends
562 Camp Horne Rd., Ohio Twp.
(412) 847-7000
www.animal-friends.org

Animal Rescue League
6620 Hamilton Ave., East Liberty
(412) 661-6452
www.animalrescue.org

**Western Pennsylvania
Humane Society**
1101 Western Ave., North Side
(412) 321-4625
www.wpahumane.org

Pet-Friendly Parks:

Frick Park
Hartwood Acres Off-Leash Park
Highland Park
Schenley Park

Pet Resources:

www.dogster.com
www.fostercat.org
www.peoplewithpets.com
www.petfinder.com
www.pghdogs.com
www.pittsburghveterinarians.com

Being Green in Pittsburgh

Pittsburgh has come a long way since its "hell with the lid off" days, and the city continues to increase its commitment to the environment. Recycling is mandatory for every resident, business, and institution in the city. Newspapers, plastic, glass, and metal are picked up curbside biweekly, and there are drop-off centers throughout the city.

Bike Pittsburgh noted a 37 percent increase in residents commuting to work by bike in 2007, and more and more Zipcar spaces are showing up within the city. Organizations like Upcycle Art are working hard to raise awareness of more conscious and creative uses of resources, and the East End's Construction Junction promotes conservation through the sale of recycled and surplus building materials.

Pittsburgh's David L. Lawrence Convention Center, the world's largest green building, is just one of 40 buildings that are either certified or registered under the U.S. Green Building Counsel's LEED rating system, giving Pittsburgh the largest and most diverse collection of green buildings in the country.

Organizations to Join

Pittsburgh Cares

www.pittsburghcares.org

Pittsburgh Cares is an umbrella organization for volunteers in the city. The organization helps people find out about volunteer needs in Pittsburgh.

Pittsburgh Urban Magnet Project (PUMP)

www.pump.org

PUMP is a local organization that encourages civic engagement, community development, and social networking.

Places to Volunteer

Americorps, Big Brothers Big Sisters, Children's Hospital, Cyert Center for Early Education, Habitat for Humanity, Humane Society, Peddle Pittsburgh, the American Red Cross, Special Olympics, United Mitochondrial Disease Foundation, United Way

Locals Speak Out On...
Lifestyles

> "There is no better city for the standard of living—it's affordable and has great hospitals and great suburban schools."

Q "Pittsburgh is a great place to have a family. **It's urban without being overwhelming**. The city has some of the best education to offer. You can enroll your child into the city schools or one of the many private ones."

Q "**Pittsburgh is pretty pet friendly**. If you live in the suburbs, it's almost code to have a dog."

Q "I don't think Pittsburgh is great for starting a family. The schools aren't that great unless you want to enroll them into a private facility. **I would recommend that you have fun then move when you're ready for a family**."

Q "On the whole, Pittsburgh is not very green. Your average Pittsburgher is not particularly environmentally conscious. That said, **the environmental movement in Pittsburgh, though small, is strong and vocal**. There are signs that people's awareness is starting to change. One big drawback of Pittsburgh with respect to greenness is the lack of space for bikers on city streets."

Q "The suburbs are best for families. Crafton is a great neighborhood for starting a family. **We have a lot of young families here**."

Q "Big Brothers Big Sisters is huge in the city. **They do a great job and are very involved in the community**. That's a great organization here in the city. There are also plenty of animal shelters to get involved with."

Q "Pittsburgh was voted 'America's Most Livable City' probably because the cost of living is extremely low. **You can rent and buy for significantly less** than in cities like New York or Washington, D.C."

Q "**It is possible for pet owners to find sympathetic landlords if they just look around**. Most landlords will agree to allow pets for an additional deposit. There are plenty of veterinary offices in the area and lots of animal shelters that do great work."

Q "**You'll be able to afford a nice house** to raise your children in, and there are lots of kid-friendly activities here."

Q "I loved having my dogs in the city. **There are trails and parks for walking and more grass than most cities**."

Q "It's a fantastic place to have a family. The cost of living is very low, so you can rent or buy in the city. **There are many family-friendly neighborhoods**. Pitt Daycare is the best in the city, but Carriage House and CMU day care are great, too."

Q "I grew up in the suburbs of the city, and **I would definitely raise my children here**."

Q "**Pittsburgh is a great city for young families**. Housing is affordable, and there are great parks and recreation facilities throughout the city."

Q "We just started our family and one of the best things about Pittsburgh is that they have a freestanding birth center called The Midwife Center in the Strip District. **Top-notch midwifery care!**"

Q "My parents started our family in Pittsburgh, and we haven't moved. **It's pretty much an awesome place to grow up**."

The Urban Guru Take On...
Lifestyles

After receiving the title of "America's Most Livable City" by *Places Rated Almanac* for the second time, it's undeniable that there are plenty of good reasons to live in Pittsburgh. Young professionals and families just starting out will appreciate the low cost of living compared to that of other cities of similar size. With the cost of living more than 16 percent lower than the national average, starting a family and buying a home in Pittsburgh is realistic and plausible. For young families, childcare options are readily available. The city offers a variety of family-friendly destinations and is increasingly pet-friendly.

Home to a variety of social and nonprofit organizations, museums, sports teams, and cultural attractions, Pittsburgh offers residents a variety of activities in the city. Beautiful parks, including Schenley, Frick, and Highland, offer residents the chance to appreciate nature, stay active, and walk pets—all located near some of the most popular neighborhoods. An increasing effort, though still gaining momentum, is encouraging more proactive and environmentally conscious citizens. With an increasing number of Pittsburghers thinking "green," there has been an influx of residents choosing to bike to work or find alternative modes of transportation.

The Urban Guru® Grade on
Lifestyles: A

A high Lifestyles grade indicates that the city is affordable, pet-friendly, and a good place to raise a family. Other determining factors include how environmentally friendly the city is and how involved residents can become in the community.

Employment

The Lowdown On...
Employment

Median Family Income:
$47,658

Unemployment Rate:
4.9%

Overall Job Growth Since 2000:
2.0% (U.S. overall: 6.2%)

Local Income Taxes:
City of Pittsburgh: 3.00%
Other Municipalities: 1.00%

Fastest-Growing Job Markets:
Construction & manufacturing
Education
Health care
Information technology
Natural resources & mining
Professional & business services

Employment Resources:
www.imaginemynewjob.com
pittsburgh.jobing.com
www.pittsburghjobs.com

➜

Pittsburgh's Largest Employers:

Bank of New York Mellon Corp.
Carnegie Mellon University
Eat'n Park Hospitality Group
Giant Eagle Inc.
Highmark Inc.
The PNC Financial Services Group
University of Pittsburgh
UPMC Health System
U.S. Steel Corp.
West Penn Allegheny
Health System
Verizon Communications

Other Places to Check Out:

Consol Energy
Dick's Sporting Goods Inc.
Federated Investors
FedEx Ground
Kennametal Inc.
LANXESS Corp.
MEDRAD Inc.
Philips Respironics Inc.

Fortune 1000 Companies Headquartered in the Pittsburgh Region

Allegheny Energy
This investor-owned utility has annual revenues of more than $3 billion and more than 4,000 employees. It provides electric service to more than 1.5 million customers in Pennsylvania, Maryland, Virginia, and West Virginia.

Allegheny Technologies
Multinational producers of stainless steel and specialty metals and one of the few remaining companies that helped make Pittsburgh the "Steel City." With headquarters downtown, it is still one of the largest employers in the county.

American Eagle Outfitters
This popular retail apparel chain recently relocated its headquarters from Marshall, Pa., to the trendy and growing SouthSide Works shopping district, employing more than 600 people.

CONSOL Energy
The largest producer of high-BTU bituminous coal in the United States, CONSOL has annual revenues of nearly $4 billion. Its head office is located just outside of Pittsburgh in Canonsburg.

Dick's Sporting Goods
A major U.S. sporting goods retailer, Dick's is headquartered in Findlay Township and has more than 350 stores in 38 states. The company generated revenues of $3.8 billion in 2007.

H.J. Heinz
Heinz is a $10 billion global company with more than 32,000 employees worldwide founded and headquartered in Pittsburgh. The corporate office is in PPG Place downtown.

Kennametal Inc.
This tool production company, which is headquartered in Latrobe, about 50 miles from Pittsburgh, specializes in the manufacture of products for high-tech industries.

Mylan Laboratories Inc.
The second-largest generic pharmaceutical company in the United States, Mylan has about 13,000 employees worldwide and revenues of more than $4 billion. Its headquarters are in Canonsburg, south of Pittsburgh.

The PNC Financial Services Group
On top of operating thousands of bank branches and ATMs in eight states, PNC is also one of the nation's largest financial services companies with $143 billion in assets. It is Pittsburgh's third-largest employer with 7,400 employees.

PPG Industries
An $11 billion global glass and chemicals manufacturer. Its headquarters is located downtown in PPG Place (a popular Pittsburgh landmark in its own right).

U.S. Steel Corp.
Formerly known as USX, it is the largest domestically owned steel producer in the nation and one of the largest in the world. Its headquarters downtown is also the largest skyscraper in Pittsburgh, the U.S. Steel Tower.

(Fortune 1000 Companies, continued)

WESCO International Inc.
A multinational electronics distribution and services company. Originally a part of Westinghouse, WESCO is now an independent, publicly traded company with more than 7,000 employees and $5.3 billion in sales.

Other Companies Headquartered in Pittsburgh

Alcoa, Bayer USA, Calgon Carbon Corp., Duquesne Light, Eat 'n' Park Hospitality Group Inc., Eaton Electrical, Education Management Corp., Federated Investors Inc., FedEx Ground, General Nutrition Center (GNC), Giant Eagle, GlaxoSmithKline, Highmark Inc., LANXESS Corp., MEDRAD Inc., Nova Chemicals, Philips Respironics, Siemens Water Technologies, TRACO, Union Switch and Signal, WABTEC, Westinghouse Electric Co.

Did You Know?

BusinessWeek recently ranked Pittsburgh as the **sixth best city for riding out a recession** based on the unemployment rate and the percentage of jobs in strong industries like education and health care.

Beverage cans were opened by can opener until 1962 when local company **Alcoa, a major aluminum producer, developed the pull-tab**, which first appeared on cans of Iron City beer from the Pittsburgh Brewing Company.

ImagineMyNewJob.com connects users to **more than 20,000 jobs in the Pittsburgh area** in industries like accounting, architecture, engineering, health care, information technology, life sciences, manufacturing, and more.

Salary Breakdown

These are the average salaries in Pittsburgh by job type and how those salaries stack up against the national average.

Job Category	Average Salary	% of Nat'l Avg.
Management, Business, & Financial	$62,633	94%
Professional & Related	$50,881	95%
Installation, Maintenance, & Repair	$40,740	97%
Transportation & Material Moving	$36,863	95%
Construction & Extraction	$36,261	98%
Production & Manufacturing	$34,807	98%
Sales & Related	$32,759	90%
Office/Administrative Support	$30,841	97%
Service Positions	$24,576	96%

Cost of Living Comparisons

This list shows how other U.S. cities of various sizes stack up to Pittsburgh in terms of cost of living and average salary.

City	Cost of Living	Average Salary
Baltimore	6% higher	6% higher
Buffalo, N.Y.	4% lower	1% higher
Chicago	16% higher	9% higher
Cincinnati	4% lower	1% higher
Cleveland	1% higher	3% higher
Los Angeles	31% higher	12% higher
New York	42% higher	17% higher
Philadelphia	15% higher	8% higher
Richmond, Va.	1% lower	1% higher
Seattle	14% higher	11% higher
Washington, D.C.	35% higher	10% higher

Locals Speak Out On...
Employment

{ **"Pittsburgh has a lot of opportunities, and putting the effort into multiple interviews and job offers is worth the time. There are a lot of significant publicly traded companies in the area."**

Q "Jobs downtown tend to pay more than those in the suburbs on the outskirts. **There aren't that many jobs in graphic design available at most times**. There are usually one or two listed when I do look."

Q "**Use the career agencies Pittsburgh has to offer**, as well as classified advertising in Craigslist, the *Tribune Review*, and the *Post-Gazette*."

Q "Marketing opportunities are limited in this city, but because of that, if you get an 'in,' then you have the potential to make a greater splash. In general, Pittsburgh would be **a good place to start a new business because of low rent**. It depends on the type of business, though. Several attempts are made to make Pittsburgh seem high-end, but the city doesn't quite identify with that."

Q "There are many jobs available in Pittsburgh; however, **you may have to settle for a job outside of the industry you were hoping for**, based on the type of city it is. I was very lucky that my industry has a headquarters in Pittsburgh."

Q "I took a promotion with my company to move here. There are several opportunities in the insurance industry. But **in this economy, it's going to be difficult anywhere** to start a new business."

Q "**Seek out a headhunter**—they usually are a great channel for helping you find a job in the local area."

Q "I work 45 minutes east of the city. There are lots of opportunities in the health care field because of the abundance of hospitals. **UPMC generally has many openings in my field** (athletic training), as well as other aspects of health care."

Q "**There are plenty of jobs in the accounting field** and a low cost of living."

Q "**I stayed in Pittsburgh because there were good job opportunities that met my career goals**. As an accountant, I think that there are a lot of job opportunities in my field in both public accounting and private industry. I feel that there is a lot of flexibility in my field, and I have the ability to tailor my career to my objectives and goals. The accounting field can be competitive, but if you have a CPA and some experience, the job-search process is not too bad. You may not get the first job that you interview for due to the competition, but it is likely you will find one that meets your needs. I am very happy with my career opportunities thus far."

Q "I chose to stay here for my kids and because I find the nightlife and cultural scene to be great—not New York City, of course, but not small-town America. I eventually started my own consulting business, and it's been great. **There seem to be a lot of DIY businesses**, so I'm assuming the atmosphere is good for others as well."

Q "I chose to work here because of **the many great opportunities that the city offers for nurses**."

Q "I grew up here. **When the steel industry collapsed, it had a big effect on jobs in the area**, but the city has remade itself. We need to draw more young people in and provide more jobs for them so the area thrives."

Q "Because it's a smaller city, **employers usually rely on their own Web sites for job recruitment**, so go that route. Also, you probably know someone who is from Pittsburgh or has a contact in Pittsburgh, so get a name to contact directly."

Q "For a graphic design graduate, there is just nothing here. **I make copies at a copy shop with my bachelor's degree**. I do want to start my own business soon, but I haven't done much with it yet, so I'm not sure if it's a good place or not. I definitely can't find freelance to help me get started."

Q "Pittsburgh is a good place to start a business because of **the city's push to build new businesses in the area**. There are many funds available to seed early-stage startups. Every university offers help for their alums to get their startup off the ground. You can easily find financial help for your startup in the area if you look hard enough."

Q "I'm a teacher, and this is **one of the best areas for teaching**, so that's why I stayed. I think that the city would be a good place to start a business, depending on what it is."

Q "Definitely check out Craigslist. That's where I found my current job, and it seems like a lot of companies post there. Also, be willing to take a pay cut. If you're coming from an area with a higher cost of living, **the salaries here may seem really low to you**, but remember, the cost of living here is ridiculously low. You can buy a decent house for around $100,000."

Q "Jobs can be a problem here. I had a hard time finding one when I first moved here with a year's worth of experience under my belt. Talk to a placement agency, who will sometimes have leads on jobs that aren't advertised, and **work any connections you have**."

Q "**I chose to move back to Pittsburgh because of the availability of jobs**—specifically the one that I was offered. The pay is better than I ever expected, and they have benefits competitive with other areas."

Q "Quality marketing positions are very difficult to find in Pittsburgh. **There is a lot of competition and not a lot of opportunities**. Unfortunately a lot of the 'marketing' positions listed on job Web sites are bogus."

Q "I wouldn't call the job market in Pittsburgh 'hot,' but **it's definitely easier to find a job in certain fields**, such as health care, technology, and higher education. There aren't many opportunities here in the editing field, but there are two large newspapers, several magazines, and corporate communications jobs."

The Urban Guru Take On...
Employment

Pittsburgh's job market has been in a state of transition for the past few decades. Pittsburgh, and Western Pennsylvania as a whole, was hit hard when the nation's steel industry collapsed in the 1980s. Fortunately, a solid base of world-class health care and research facilities, as well as the expansion of high-tech fields like information technology, advanced manufacturing, and cyber security, has helped the region to begin growing once again, and there are more job openings here now than at any other time in the region's history.

In addition to the booming tech industry, the presence of several Fortune 500 companies and major universities like Carnegie Mellon, Pitt, and Duquesne keep Pittsburgh's education and financial job markets strong, and new commercial building projects continue to create construction jobs. Pittsburgh's greatest challenges to continued growth lie in convincing its degree-holding job-seekers to stay in the region and encouraging more educated professionals to migrate in from other areas.

The Urban Guru® Grade on
Employment: B-

A high grade for Employment indicates that quality jobs are available, that strong industries are growing, and that unemployment is low. Other factors include how salaries and cost of living compare to national averages.

Education

The Lowdown On...
Education

Public School Districts:
More than 40 in
Allegheny County

Local Private Schools:
More than 200 in
Western Pennsylvania

Local Colleges and Universities:
More than 40 in the tri-state area (Eastern Ohio, West Virginia, Western Pennsylvania)

Best Public Schools:
Fox Chapel
North Allegheny
Mt. Lebanon
Upper St. Clair

Best Private Schools:
The Ellis School
Sewickley Academy
Shadyside Academy
Winchester Thurston School

→

Public School Districts:

Avonworth
258 Josephs Ln., Avonworth
(412) 369-8738
www.avonworth.k12.pa.us
Millage: 18.8
District Enrollment: 1,346
Graduation Rate: 97.87%
SAT Scores: 522 verbal/517 math

Baldwin-Whitehall
4900 Curry Rd., Baldwin
(412) 884-6300
www.bwschools.net
Millage: 23.61
District Enrollment: 4,293
Graduation Rate: 99.42%
SAT Scores: 495 verbal/508 math

Bethel Park
301 Church Rd., Bethel Park
(412) 883-5000
www.bpsd.org
Millage Rate: 23.18
District Enrollment: 5,073
Graduation Rate: 95.54%
SAT Scores: 518 verbal/537 math

Brentwood Borough
3601 Brownsville Rd., Brentwood
(412) 881-2227
brentwoodpgh.k12.pa.us
Millage: 28.27
District Enrollment: 1,327
Graduation Rate: 94.53%
SAT Scores: 484 verbal/503 math

Carlynton
435 Kings Highway, Carnegie
(412) 429-8400
www.carlynton.k12.pa.us
Millage: 24.15
District Enrollment: 1,544
Graduation Rate: 94.57%
SAT Scores: 488 verbal/515 math

Chartiers Valley
2030 Swallow Hill Rd., Scott Twp.
(412) 429-2202
www.cvsd.net
Millage: 19.32
District Enrollment: 3,428
Graduation Rate: 97.79%
SAT Scores: 497 verbal/515 math

Fox Chapel Area
611 Field Club Rd., Fox Chapel
(412) 967-2414
www.fcasd.edu
Millage: 20.3
District Enrollment: 4,581
Graduation Rate: 96.89%
SAT Scores: 547 verbal/546 math

Keystone Oaks
1000 Kelton Ave., Dormont
(412) 571-6008
www.kosd.org
Millage: 21.31
District Enrollment: 2,433
Graduation Rate: 86.23%
SAT Scores: 490 verbal/502 math

Montour

223 Clever Rd., McKees Rocks
(412) 490-6500
www.montourschools.com
Millage: 18.9
District Enrollment: 3,174
Graduation Rate: 98.41%
SAT Scores: 488 verbal/491 math

Mt. Lebanon

7 Horsman Dr., Mt. Lebanon
(412) 344-2077
www.mtlsd.org
Millage: 23.81
District Enrollment: 5,441
Graduation Rate: 99.59%
SAT Scores: 568 verbal/573 math

North Allegheny

200 Hillvue Ln., Pittsburgh
(412) 369-5430
www.northallegheny.org
Millage: 18.99
District Enrollment: 8,045
Graduation Rate: 100%
SAT Scores: 555 verbal/569 math

North Hills

135 Sixth Ave., North Hills
(412) 318-1017
www.nhsd.net
Millage: 19.6
District Enrollment: 4,771
Graduation Rate: 96.44%
SAT Scores: 514 verbal/526 math

Northgate

591 Union Ave., Bellevue
(412) 732-3300
www.northgate.k12.pa.us
Millage: 24.5
District Enrollment: 1,428
Graduation Rate: 89.26%
SAT Scores: 460 verbal/465 math

Penn Hills

309 Collins Dr., Penn Hills
(412) 793-7000
www.phsd.k12.pa.us
Millage: 24.81
District Enrollment: 5,490
Graduation Rate: 93.36%
SAT Scores: 470 verbal/470 math

Pittsburgh Public Schools

341 S. Bellefield Ave., Pittsburgh
(412) 622-3500
www.pghboe.net
Millage: 13.92
District Enrollment: 24,236
Avg. Graduation Rate: 84.17%
SAT Avg.: 439 verbal/438 math

Plum Borough

200 School Rd., Plum
(412) 795-0100
www.pbsd.k12.pa.us
Millage: 22.2
District Enrollment: 4,387
Graduation Rate: 96.49%
SAT Scores: 483 verbal/496 math

Quaker Valley
203 Graham St., Sewickley
(412) 749-3600
www.qvsd.org
Millage: 19.75
District Enrollment: 1,912
Graduation Rate: 98.71%
SAT Scores: 529 verbal/555 math

Riverview
701 10th St., Oakmont
(412) 828-1800
www.rsd.k12.pa.us
Millage: 23.11
District Enrollment: 1,209
Graduation Rate: 97%
SAT Scores: 501 verbal/513 math

Shaler Area
1800 Mt. Royal Blvd., Glenshaw
(412) 492-1200
sasd.k12.pa.us
Millage: 24.7
District Enrollment: 5,491
Graduation Rate: 97.63%
SAT Scores: 493 verbal/500 math

South Allegheny
2743 Washington Blvd.
McKeesport
(412) 675-3070
www.southallegheny.org
Millage: 18.11
District Enrollment: 1,710
Graduation Rate: 93.15%
SAT Scores: 463 verbal/455 math

South Fayette Township
3660 Old Oakdale Rd., McDonald
(412) 221-4542
www.southfayette.org
Millage: 24.04
District Enrollment: 1,982
Graduation Rate: 98.11%
SAT Scores: 511 verbal/536 math

South Park
2005 Eagle Ridge, South Park
(412) 655-3111
www.sparksd.org
Millage: 25.99
District Enrollment: 2,217
Graduation Rate: 95.43%
SAT Scores: 497 verbal/522 math

Steel Valley
220 E. Oliver Rd., Munhall
(412) 464-3600
www.svsd.k12.pa.us
Millage: 21.21
District Enrollment: 2,096
Graduation Rate: 86.84%
SAT Scores: 463 verbal/475 math

Sto-Rox
600 Russellwood, McKees Rocks
(412) 771-3213
www.srsd.k12.pa.us
Millage: 25.00
District Enrollment: 1,447
Graduation Rate: 80.47%
SAT Scores: 412 verbal/424 math

Upper St. Clair
1820 McLaughlin Run, Pittsburgh
(412) 833-1600
www.uscsd.k12.pa.us
Millage: 22.45
District Enrollment: 4,109
Graduation Rate: 99.73%
SAT Scores: 565 verbal/579 math

West Jefferson Hills
835 Old Clairton, Jefferson Hills
(412) 655-8450
www.wjhsd.net
Millage: 21.08
District Enrollment: 2,844
Graduation Rate: 97.19%
SAT Scores: 501 verbal/516 math

West Mifflin Area
3000 Lebanon Church Rd.
West Mifflin
(412) 466-9131
www.wmasd.org
Millage: 22.292
District Enrollment: 3,238
Graduation Rate: 96.85%
SAT Scores: 459 verbal/466 math

Wilkinsburg Borough
718 Wallace Ave., Wilkinsburg
(412) 371-9667
www.wilkinsburgschools.org
Millage: 35.00
District Enrollment: 1,546
Graduation Rate: 85.44%
SAT Scores: 362 verbal/375 math

Woodland Hills
2430 Greensburg Pike, Churchill
(412) 731-1300
www.whsd.k12.pa.us
Millage: 24.65
District Enrollment: 5,342
Graduation Rate: 80.28%
SAT Scores: 462 verbal/459 math

Private Schools:

Bishop Canevin High School
2700 Morange Rd., Crafton
(412) 922-7400
www.bishopcanevin.org
Enrollment: 483 (9–12)
Student/Teacher Ratio: 16:1

Central Catholic High School
4720 Fifth Ave., Oakland
(412) 621-8189
www.pittcentralcatholic.org
Enrollment: 832 (9–12; all boys)
Student/Teacher Ratio: 15:1

The Ellis School
6425 Fifth Ave., Point Breeze
(412) 661-5992
www.theellisschool.org
Enrollment: 486 (K–12; all girls)
Student/Teacher Ratio: 6:1

The Kiski School
1888 Brett Ln., Saltsburg
(877) 547-5448
www.kiski.org

(The Kiski School, continued)
Enrollment: 206 (9–12; all boys)
Student/Teacher Ratio: 7:1

North Catholic High School
1400 Troy Hill Rd., Troy Hill
(412) 321-4823
www.north-catholic.org
Enrollment: 290 (9–12)
Student/Teacher Ratio: 14:1

Oakland Catholic High School
144 N. Craig St., Oakland
(412) 682-6633
www.oaklandcatholic.org
Enrollment: 543 (9–12; all girls)
Student/Teacher Ratio: 12:1

The Oakland School
362 McKee Pl., Oakland
(412) 621-7878
www.theoaklandschool.org
Enrollment: 70 (8–12)
Student/Teacher Ratio: 6:1

Serra Catholic High School
200 Hershey Dr., McKeesport
(412) 751-2020
www.serrahs.org
Enrollment: (310; 9–12)
Student/Teacher Ratio: 12:1

Seton-LaSalle High School
1000 McNeilly Rd., Mt. Lebanon
(412) 561-3583
www.slshs.org

(Seton-LaSalle, continued)
Enrollment: 541 (9–12)
Student/Teacher Ratio: 14:1

Sewickley Academy
315 Academy Ave., Sewickley
(412) 741-2230
www.sewickley.org
Enrollment: 800 (K–12)
Student/Teacher Ratio: 9:1

Shady Side Academy
423 Fox Chapel Rd., Fox Chapel
(412) 968-3000
www.shadysideacademy.org
Enrollment: 918 (K–12)
Student/Teacher Ratio: 9:1

St. Edmund's Academy
5705 Darlington Rd., Squirrel Hill
(412) 521-1907
www.stedmunds.net
Enrollment: 270 (K–8)
Student/Teacher Ratio: 7:1

Trinity Christian School
299 Ridge Ave., Forest Hills
(412) 242-8886
www.trinitychristian.net
Enrollment: 326 (K–12)
Student/Teacher Ratio: 12:1

Vincentian Academy
Peebles Rd. at McKnight Rd.,
North Hills
(412) 364-1616

(Vincentian, continued)
www.vaduq.org
Enrollment: 240 (9–12)
Student/Teacher Ratio: 14:1

Waldorf School of Pittsburgh
201 S. Winebiddle St., Friendship
(412) 441-5792
waldorfpittsburgh.org
Enrollment: 87 (K–5)
Student/Teacher Ratio: 10:1

Winchester Thurston School
555 Morewood Ave., Shadyside
(412) 578-7500
www.winchesterthurston.org
Enrollment: 625 (K–12)
Student/Teacher Ratio: 7:1

Yeshiva Schools of Pittsburgh
2100 Wightman St., Squirrel Hill
(412) 422-7300
www.yeshivaschool.org
Enrollment: 129 (K–12)
Student/Teacher Ratio: 8:1

Did You Know?

The Pittsburgh Public School District includes:
- 39 **early childhood** centers for ages 3–5;
- 27 neighborhood elementary schools, four **neighborhood middle schools**, and eight neighborhood high schools;
- 8 **accelerated-learning academies** serving grades K–8, one gifted center, and four special education centers; and
- 15 magnet schools/programs serving grades K–8 and eight **magnet schools/programs** for grades 9–12.

Best Pittsburgh Public High Schools:

Allderdice	SAT Avg.: 1086	Grad. Rate: 96.10%
CAPA	SAT Avg.: 1000	Grad. Rate: 97.25%
Schenley	SAT Avg.: 939	Grad. Rate: 90.53%

Worst Pittsburgh Public High Schools:

Oliver	SAT Avg.: 729	Grad. Rate: 81.75%
Westinghouse	SAT Avg.: 739	Grad. Rate: 81.25%
Langley	SAT Avg.: 830	Grad. Rate: 66.87%

Local Colleges and Universities:

Art Institute of Pittsburgh
420 Blvd. of the Allies, Downtown
(800) 275-2470
www.artinstitutes.edu/pittsburgh

California Univ. of Pennsylvania
250 University Ave., California
(724) 938-4404
www.cup.edu

Carlow University
3333 Fifth Ave., Oakland
(800) 333-2275
www.carlow.edu

Carnegie Mellon University
5000 Forbes Ave., Oakland
(412) 268-2082
www.cmu.edu

Chatham University
Woodland Road, Point Breeze
(800) 837-1290
www.chatham.edu

Clarion University
840 Wood St., Clarion
(800) 672-7171
www.clarion.edu

Duquesne University
600 Forbes Ave., Uptown
(800) 456-0590
www.duq.edu

Geneva College
3200 College Ave., Beaver
(800) 847-8255
www.geneva.edu

Grove City College
100 Campus Dr., Grove City
(724) 458-2000
www.gcc.edu

Indiana University of Pennsylvania
1011 South Dr., Indiana
(724) 357-2100
www.iup.edu

La Roche College
9000 Babcock Blvd., North Hills
(800) 838-4572
www.laroche.edu

Penn State Branch Campuses
100 University Dr., Monaca
(877) JOIN-PSU
www.beaver.psu.edu
One University Dr., Uniontown
(724) 430-4100
www.fe.psu.edu
4000 University Dr., McKeesport
(800) 248-LION
www.ga.psu.edu
3550 7th St. Rd., New Kensington
(888) 968-PAWS
www.nk.psu.edu

Point Park University
201 Wood St., Downtown
(800) 321-0129
www.pointpark.edu

Robert Morris University
6001 University Blvd., Moon Twp.
(800) 763-0097
www.rmu.edu

Seton Hill University
Seton Hill Drive, Greensburg
(800) 826-6234
www.setonhill.edu

Slippery Rock University
1 Morrow Way, Slippery Rock
(800) SRU-9111
www.sru.edu

St. Vincent College
300 Fraser Purchase Rd.
Latrobe
(800) 782-5549
www.stvincent.edu

University of Pittsburgh
4227 Fifth Ave., Oakland
(412) 624-7488
www.pitt.edu

**University of Pittsburgh
at Greensburg**
Greensburg-Mt. Pleasant Road,
Greensburg
(724) 836-9880
www.upg.pitt.edu

**Washington &
Jefferson College**
60 S. Lincoln St., Washington
(724) 223-6025
www.washjeff.edu

Waynesburg University
51 W. College St., Waynesburg
(800) 225-7393
www.waynesburg.edu

West Virginia University
University Avenue,
Morgantown, W.V.
(800) 344-9881
www.wvu.edu

Did You Know?

Pittsburgh ranks ninth among the top 10 most literate cities in the United States based on bookstores, educational attainment, newspaper circulation, periodical publishing resources, and library and Internet resources. Pittsburgh has ranked in the top 10 since the study originated in 2003.

Locals Speak Out On...
Education

"I came here for grad school knowing nothing about the city. I ended up changing careers so I could stay in Pittsburgh because I fell in love with this place. It's a city where I can enjoy raising a family and being young and successful."

Q "Pittsburgh has fantastic universities. The big three are the University of Pittsburgh, Duquesne University, and Carnegie Mellon University. The city is a great size for those attending college and just out of college. **It's large enough to explore and find opportunity** but small enough that networking can work and experience can be gained."

Q "I attended Oakland Catholic, an all-girls private high school. Though the Pittsburgh School District itself doesn't have the best reputation, there are several good public schools in outlying areas. **The private schools in the city have very good reputations on the whole,** but the tuition at these schools varies greatly—some cost a few thousand dollars a year, while others are comparable to a year at a pricey college."

Q "The only element of the city that helped to influence my decision to attend Carnegie Mellon University was the **abundance of arts and museums** that are easily available to students."

Q "**Pittsburgh is the perfect city to attend college in**. The city atmosphere has so much to offer college students as far as activities and events are concerned, but because Pittsburgh isn't too large, it is still very manageable and easy to grow accustomed to."

Q "I went to Penn Trafford High School, and I stayed here because I didn't really have any intentions to go anywhere else. **The schools here are fantastic**. Of the public schools, check out Gateway, Mt. Lebanon, Baldwin, West Mifflin, North Allegheny, East Allegheny, and Pittsburgh Public Schools. On the private front, look into North Catholic, Oakland Catholic, and Central Catholic. These are just a few, but they are all very good schools."

Q "I graduated from Carnegie Mellon University in 2002. The city of Pittsburgh was a big part of the reason I went to CMU. **It's a blue-collar city with a lot of pride**, and it's a very down-to-earth city. Nobody I've met from Pittsburgh ever thinks they are above or better than anyone else."

Q "**Shadyside Academy is a good private school**. Fox Chapel, Mt. Lebanon, and Upper St. Clair are the best school districts."

Q "I knew I wanted to go to school in an urban environment, and Carnegie Mellon offered me the best financial aid package. It is in a great location—close to Oakland, Shadyside, and Squirrel Hill, with **so much in the way of shopping and cultural opportunities**."

Q "I went to Citizen's School of Nursing in New Kensington, and I stayed around the area because I knew that there were so many opportunities. I know a lot of people who have raised kids in the city, and **many of them have sent their kids to private schools** because the city schools leave a lot to be desired."

Q "I think North Hills is a solid school district. My graduating class had about 400 students. I was prepared for college, and there was a good mix of people and community. Some other local schools like North Allegheny have a more dominant reputation, but the classes are much larger (around 800), and **students can get lost in the shuffle**."

Q "Upper St. Clair is a great school district, but **there is nothing to do if you live there**. It's too far removed from everything."

Q "Pittsburgh has some very good public education. Some of the **best districts in the state** are scattered around Pittsburgh. There are some very good private schools, but they are not necessary if you are in the right area of town."

Q "The city played a major part in my decision to go to the Art Institute of Pittsburgh. **It's a big city, but it's not overwhelming**. If you plan to attend AIP, talk to some students before making the decision. There are mixed feelings about the curriculum and instructors."

Q "The city has a number of good schools and **a strong set of magnet schools**."

Q "Pittsburgh has great higher-education opportunities. The colleges and universities here are top notch. Pitt is a gem, and Duquesne, Chatham, Carlow, and Point Park are all good schools. The best public school districts are North Allegheny, Mt. Lebanon, and Fox Chapel. **Pittsburgh city schools are pretty decent for a city district**, but try to get your kids into one of the magnet schools. Private schools, such as Ellis, Winchester-Thurston, Shadyside Academy, and Sewickley Academy, are all very good. The Catholic schools have a good reputation as well, particularly Central Catholic (for boys)."

Q "Central Catholic is an excellent school. **Ninety-six percent of my graduating class went off to college**."

Q "I went to the Art Institute of Pittsburgh. When I first visited, I fell in love with the city and its history. I just didn't know that the city was destroying its history (Fort Pitt) and that **the majority of men were self-centered, egotistical jerks** obsessed with beer, football, and big-boobed women."

Q "Two private schools, **Shadyside Academy and Sewickley Academy, seem to dominate** the area. North Hills area school districts, such as Hampton and North Allegheny, enjoy very good reputations. Other very good districts in the south include Mt. Lebanon and Upper St. Clair."

Q "I chose to go to Point Park University because **I loved the 'little big city' atmosphere**."

Q "I graduated from Upper St. Clair High School. I would definitely **recommend this school district to anyone moving into the area**. It is considered one of the best schools in the state. The graduation rate is almost 100 percent, and I would say about 95 percent of the students who graduate end up attending college."

Q "Basically all private or parochial schools are good in the area. **Most school districts in the north or south are ranked among the highest in the state**."

Q "Suburban public schools are obviously better, as in most if not all cities. **There is a plethora of excellent private schools that are worth noting**, like The Ellis School for girls, Winchester Thurston School, and Shadyside Academy."

Q "Based on what I've seen and heard, most of the top schools in the area are in the suburbs—Mt. Lebanon, Hampton, Upper St. Clair, Fox Chapel. In the city, Allderdice is a very good high school, but the rest are poor at best, so **you need to be careful where you choose to live if you have school-age kids**. This is one of the reasons why housing prices are so much higher in Squirrel Hill than other city neighborhoods."

The Urban Guru Take On...
Education

Pittsburgh is the largest public school district in Allegheny County and second-largest in Pennsylvania. In addition to its neighborhood schools, the district also operates magnet schools and programs offering specialized education in areas like business, creative and performing arts, foreign language, and math and science. In addition to the Pittsburgh School District, there are more than 40 local school districts within a 20-mile radius, many of which are ranked highest in the state. There is also a wealth of options in private schools—there are more than 250 private elementary and high schools in the region, both religious and secular.

Pittsburgh has an abundance of excellent colleges and universities offering basic and advanced degrees in a range of in-demand specialties, including computer science, engineering, health care, law, and marketing. There are also several area trade schools providing specialized technical training in everything from business to culinary arts. No matter what your level of education, Pittsburgh certainly has the resources you need—the city has approximately 50 percent more libraries than the national average. The Carnegie Library of Pittsburgh has 18 neighborhood branches in addition to its main branch in Oakland, and it boasts more than 3 million books and other items in circulation.

The Urban Guru® Grade on
Education: B+

A high Education grade generally indicates the availability of quality public schools, as well as a plethora of local private schools and colleges and universities to choose from.

Health & Safety

The Lowdown On...
Health & Safety

City Crime Statistics (per 100,000):

Criminal Homicide: 18.3

Rape: 41.3

Robberies (total): 511.2

Drug Violations (total): 991.1

DUI: 371.9

National Ranking:

According to the FBI Uniform Crime reports, Pittsburgh is listed as one of the five safest large cities in the United States.

Police Bureau:

Pittsburgh Bureau of Police

1203 Western Ave., North Side

(412) 323-7800

www.city.pittsburgh.pa.us/police

Police Zones:

Pittsburgh is divided into six police zones by neighborhood.

Zone 1 Police Station
1501 Brighton Rd., North Side
(412) 323-7201
Includes: North Side

Zone 2 Police Station
2000 Centre Ave., Hill District
(412) 255-2827
Includes: Downtown, Lawrenceville, Strip District

Zone 3 Police Station
1725 Mary St., South Side
(412) 488-8326
Includes: Brookline, Carrick, Mt. Washington, South Side

Zone 4 Police Station
5858 Northumberland St.
(412) 422-6520
Includes: Oakland, Point Breeze, Shadyside, and Squirrel Hill

Zone 5 Police Station
1401 Washington Blvd.
(412) 665-3605
Includes: Bloomfield, Friendship, Highland Park, and East Liberty

Zone 6 Police Station
Special Deployment Division
312 S. Main St.
(412) 937-3051
Includes: Carnegie, Crafton, Sheraden, West End

Health Care Systems:

Pittsburgh is home to world-class health care systems, including the University of Pittsburgh Medical Center (UPMC) and West Penn Allegheny Health System.

Hospitals in the Region:
32

Pittsburghers Covered by a Health Plan:
92.4%

Urgent Care Facility:

MedExpress Urgent Care

Nine locations in the Pittsburgh area

www.greatcarefast.com

Specialty Hospitals:

Children's Hospital of Pittsburgh of UPMC

Magee-Womens Hospital of UPMC

UPMC Hillman Cancer Center

Western Psychiatric Institute and Clinic

Resources for Finding a Doctor:

findadoc.upmc.com

www.alleghenycounty.net/physicians.html

www.wpahs.org/patients/physician/index.cfm

Health Care in Pittsburgh

The University of Pittsburgh Medical Center

The University of Pittsburgh Medical Center (UPMC) is the premier health care system in the region. UPMC comprises 20 tertiary, specialty, and community hospitals, 400 outpatient sites and doctors' offices, and retirement and long-term care facilities. It is also the largest employer in the city and the largest academic medical provider in the nation.

West Penn Allegheny Health System

West Penn Allegheny Health System (WPAHS) is made up of some of the oldest and best-known names in health care in western Pennsylvania, including its two tertiary care flagship hospitals and four hospitals in the suburbs.

Smoking Ban

In June 2008, Governor Ed Rendell signed into law the Clean Indoor Act, which prohibits smoking in most public places or work spaces, including bus and train stations, hospitals, restaurants, schools, sports facilities, taxis, and theaters.

Did You Know?

Pittsburgh's Medical Firsts:

- **Jonas Salk developed the first injectable polio vaccine at the University of Pittsburgh** with his team. The vaccine was first tested in 1952. On April 15, 1955, the results were announced, and the vaccine was declared safe and effective.

- **The first simultaneous heart, liver, and kidney transplant was done in Pittsburgh** at the Presbyterian-University Hospital on Dec. 3, 1989.

- In 1971, **the Pittsburgh Poison Control Center at Children's Hospital of Pittsburgh developed the Mr. Yuk sticker**. Since its creation, more than 42 million Mr. Yuk stickers have been distributed around the world, and it has remained a registered trademark of the hospital.

➡

(Did You Know? continued)

Pittsburgh's Best in the Medical World

- The University of Pittsburgh Medical Center (UPMC) is **ranked 14th among the 19 hospitals recognized as "America's Best Hospitals"** by *U.S. News & World Report*.

- In 2006, West Penn became the first and only hospital in Pittsburgh and western Pennsylvania to **achieve the prestigious Magnet recognition status** from the American Nurses Credentialing Center.

- **Children's Hospital of Pittsburgh of UPMC was one of only seven children's hospitals selected as a Top Hospital** in the country by the 2008 Leapfrog Hospital Survey, which is the nation's premier evaluation tool for patient safety.

- According to the 10th annual HealthGrades "Hospital Quality in America" study, **Allegheny General Hospital ranks among the top 10 percent in the nation for stroke care services**.

- **Magee-Womens Hospital of UPMC is ranked among the top 12 hospitals in the nation for gynecological care** and is a National Center of Excellence in Women's Health, one of the first recognized by the U.S. Department of Health and Human Services.

- Ranking among the nation's top-tier cancer institutes, the **University of Pittsburgh Cancer Institute is ranked 11th in funding from the National Cancer Institute** and 12th among *U.S. News & World Report's* 2007 "Best of the Best" cancer programs in the nation.

- Allegheny General Hospital was the region's **first hospital to receive designation as a Level I Shock Trauma Center**, which is the highest designation available. Its LifeFlight aeromedical service was the first to fly in the northeastern United States.

Locals Speak Out On...
Health & Safety

"Pittsburgh seems to have some of the best health care facilities in the country based on rankings and personal experience."

Q "Overall, I feel Pittsburgh is very safe. Like any city, there are areas to avoid. **Some of these areas are pretty close to some desirable areas of town**, but I don't feel that this element creeps into these areas."

Q "I think Pittsburgh isn't much different from other cities in terms of safety. **There are good and bad areas**."

Q "Pittsburgh has some of the best hospitals in the country, including Children's Hospital and several cancer centers. The University of Pittsburgh Medical Center is a huge asset for the city, and **many institutions are on the cutting edge of research**."

Q "I feel that Pittsburgh is relatively safe, but **I do have pepper spray on my key ring just in case**."

Q "I have been extremely impressed with the hospitals here. My husband had to go to two different ones—Mercy and Allegheny General—for emergency reasons. **I was very surprised at how nice and accommodating everyone was**."

Q "**The local police have a strong but not infringing presence and rarely are seen getting bad press**. The institution that creates the greatest havoc for citizens is the Pittsburgh Parking Authority. Those people are jerks."

Q "Pittsburgh is the city to go to for hospitals and great doctors. From my personal experiences, the doctors I have encountered are wonderful. **If you have UPMC insurance, utilize the Health Plan resources** because they offer so much information and help find information on not only doctors but also on general information on the city."

Q "I think Pittsburgh is very safe. Sure, there are areas with nightly violence, but those are mostly personal disagreements, not random acts. **Use common sense, avoid sketchy people, and stay on the beaten path** in 'bad' neighborhoods and you should be fine."

Q "**Hospitals in Pittsburgh are the best in the country**, especially given all of the specialties including pediatric and cancer research."

Q "Pittsburgh is an extremely safe city. **I've never felt uncomfortable anywhere in Pittsburgh** during the day or night. The only places that I would avoid completely are East Liberty, Garfield, Hill District, Hazelwood, and Homewood. The South Side, Lawrenceville, North Side, and Friendship can get a bit sketchy in places but are generally safe."

Q "UPMC has an excellent reputation, and **there are many locations, so it is quite convenient**."

Q "It's not the safest town. **Some areas are nice and then there could be shootings right across the street**."

Q "If you have time to wait in the emergency room, Mercy hospital is OK. Since they see some trauma patients, the wait can be a long time. If you have the option, try a **MedExpress—it might be further away, but it is quicker and more thorough**."

Q "**Just like every city, you have to be careful**. I've never been scared in the streets of South Side or Oakland, but bad things can randomly happen everywhere."

Q "The University of Pittsburgh Medical Center is nationally and world renowned and has experts in almost every field. **If you have health insurance, then you'll have no problem finding a world-class doctor or specialist** in Pittsburgh. The local dentistry and law firms are neither out of this world nor below standards, just middle of the road."

Q "**You cannot find better hospitals or doctors anywhere**! And if you are a veteran, there are many local VA facilities for your use and care."

Q "**I feel that Pittsburgh is generally a safe city**. I have been hearing about a lot of muggings going on at bus stops at night, though, which is kind of nerve racking."

Q "Hospitals and doctors are top-of-the-line. I couldn't ask for better. **Word of mouth is always the best way to get recommendations**."

Q "We haven't had any safety concerns at all. We have a home alarm system just in case, but we generally feel safe in our neighborhood. **The local police have been very responsive to petty crime around our area**."

Q "I have always felt very safe in Pittsburgh. While there are a few areas to avoid late at night, it is safe overall. There are **good and bad neighborhoods, as with any city**, and the safest areas are located outside of Downtown, like Mt. Lebanon, Cranberry, and Robinson. Shadyside and Squirrel Hill are also relatively safe."

The Urban Guru Take On...
Health & Safety

One of Pittsburgh's most notable attributes is its extensive system of world-class hospitals. With two major health care systems—University of Pittsburgh Medical Center (UPMC) and West Penn Allegheny Health System—some of the best health facilities in the country are located in Pittsburgh, from cancer centers to women's health to children's hospitals. In addition to major hospitals and facilities within the health systems, there are urgent care clinics throughout the city. MedExpress Urgent Care and Minute Clinics (located in CVS pharmacies) are alternatives for those in need of medical care who feel that the wait and care at an emergency room is not necessary.

In terms of safety, Pittsburgh has a low crime rate, ranking the lowest of the 24 largest metro areas, according to *VisitPittsburgh.com*. As in any major city, there are always areas to avoid and reasons to remain cautious. Certain neighborhoods within the city limits have a reputation for higher crime rates than others. What is interesting about Pittsburgh is that, with 90 distinct neighborhoods, the distance between a more prosperous neighborhood and one with crime issues may only be a matter of a few miles. Overall, most residents in Pittsburgh note that they have never felt threatened while living in the city and believe that the Pittsburgh Police do a fine job in maintaining a safe city.

The Urban Guru® Grade on
Health & Safety: A

A high grade in Health & Safety means that the city is safe, the crime rate is low, there is a visible police presence, the hospitals and facilities are reputable and offer a variety of general practitioners and specialists, and that there are alternative options available.

www.collegeprowler.com/urbanguru

City Dining

The Lowdown On...
City Dining

Restaurant Prowler:
Popular Places to Eat!

BREAKFAST
DeLuca's Restaurant
2015 Penn Ave., Strip District
(412) 566-2195
Price: $8–$15
Hours: Monday–Friday
6 a.m.–2:30 p.m.,
Saturday 6 a.m.–3 p.m.,
Sunday 7 a.m.–3 p.m.

Pamela's
3703 Forbes Ave., Oakland
(412) 683-4066
5527 Walnut St., Shadyside
(412) 683-1003
5813 Forbes Ave., Squirrel Hill
(412) 422-9457
60 21st St., Strip District
(412) 281-6366
Cool Features: *Pittsburgh Magazine's* Readers' Choice for best breakfast for 10 years.
Price: $5–$10
Hours: Daily 7:30 a.m.–5 p.m.

CAFÉS & COFFEEHOUSES

Beehive Coffeehouse
1327 E. Carson St., South Side
(412) 488-4483
www.beehivebuzz.com
Cool Features: The Beehive offers free Wi-Fi, great atmosphere, pinball machines
Price: $5–$15
Hours: Monday–Thursday 8 a.m.–1 a.m., Friday–Saturday 9 a.m.–2 a.m.

La Prima Espresso Bar
205 21st St., Strip District
(412) 281-1922
www.laprima.com
Cool Features: This espresso/cappuccino bar also serves breakfast and light lunches.
Price: $5–$10
Hours: Daily 6 a.m.–4 p.m.

Quiet Storm
5430 Penn Ave., Garfield
(412) 661-9355
www.quietstormcoffee.com
Cool Features: Also a vegetarian restaurant.
Price: $5–$10
Hours: Monday–Friday 8 a.m.–9 p.m., Saturday 10 a.m.–9 p.m., Sunday 10 a.m.–4 p.m.

Square Café
1137 S. Braddock Ave.
Regent Square
(412) 244-8002

(Square Café, continued)
www.square-cafe.com
Cool Features: This café serves breakfast, crepes, salads, sandwiches, and wraps.
Price: $5–$10
Hours: Monday–Saturday 7 a.m.–3 p.m., Sunday 8 a.m.–3 p.m.

The Zenith
86 S. 26th St., South Side
(412) 481-4833
www.zenithpgh.com
Cool Features: Antique shop, art gallery, and vegetarian café.
Price: $10–$15
Hours: Thursday–Saturday 11 a.m.–9 p.m., Sunday 11 a.m.–3 p.m.

Other Places to Check Out:
17th Street Café
21st Street Coffee and Tea
61C Café
Aldo Coffee
Beleza Community Coffeehouse
Buon Giorno Café
Café Cravings
Café 'n' Creamery
Coffee Tree Roasters
Crazy Mocha
Enrico's Tazza D'Oro
Jitters Café
Kiva Han
Leaf & Bean Co.
Nicholas Coffee
Point Brugge Café

www.collegeprowler.com/urbanguru

AMERICAN

Atria's Restaurant and Tavern

110 Beverly Rd., Mt. Lebanon
(412) 343-2411

103 Federal St., North Shore
(412) 322-1850

www.atrias.com

Cool Features: Seven locations.

Price: $15–$25

Hours: Monday–Thursday
11 a.m.–11 p.m., Friday–
Saturday 11 a.m.–12 a.m.,
Sunday 11 a.m.–10 p.m.

Church Brew Works

3525 Liberty Ave., Lawrenceville
(412) 688-8200

www.churchbrew.com

Cool Features: This unique
brewery and eatery is set in an
old church.

Price: $15–$30

Hours: Monday–Thursday
11:30 a.m.–11:45 p.m., Friday–
Saturday 11:30 a.m.–1 a.m.,
Sunday 12 p.m.–10 p.m.

Coal Hill Steakhouse

1212 Grandview Ave.
Mt. Washington
(412) 431-1400

www.coalhillsteakhouse.com

Cool Features: Two dining
levels and an outdoor deck
offer wonderful views.

Price: $15–$35

Hours: Sunday–Thursday
11 a.m.–10 p.m., Friday–
Saturday 11 a.m.–11 p.m.

Double Wide Grill

2339 E. Carson St., South Side
(412) 390-1111

doublewidegrill.com

Cool Features: Cool Americana
décor, outdoor dining, and lots
of vegetarian options.

Price: $10–$20

Hours: Daily 11 a.m.–2 a.m.

Eat'n Park

245 Waterfront Dr., Homestead
(412) 464-7275

www.eatnpark.com

Cool Features: Think Denny's
with a salad bar. More than 20
area locations.

Price: $10–$20

Hours: Daily 24 hours

Eleven Contemporary Kitchen

1150 Smallman St., Strip District
(412) 201-5656

www.bigburrito.com/eleven

Price: $20–$40

Hours: Monday–Thursday
11:30 a.m.–2 p.m.,
5 p.m.–10 p.m.,
Friday 11:30 a.m.–2 p.m.,
5 p.m.–11 p.m.,
Saturday 5 p.m.–11 p.m.,
Sunday 5 p.m.–9 p.m.

Fat Heads Saloon

1805 E. Carson St., South Side
(412) 431-7433

www.fatheads.com

Cool Features: Not your typical
bar food. Multiple awards

(Fat Heads Saloon, continued)
for best bar food, wings, burgers, and beer selection.
Price: $10–$20
Hours: Monday–Thursday 11 a.m.–12 a.m., Friday–Saturday 11 a.m.–1 a.m., Sunday 11 a.m.–11 p.m.

Fuel & Fuddle
214 Oakland Ave., Oakland
(412) 682-3473
www.fuelandfuddle.com
Cool Features: Serving what they call "wildfire food," F&F is a late-night favorite offering two specially brewed house beers.
Price: $15–$20
Hours: Daily 11 a.m.–2 a.m.

Gullifty's Restaurant
1922 Murray Ave., Squirrel Hill
(412) 521-8222
www.gulliftysrestaurant.com
Cool Features: Voted the city's best desserts for 20+ years.
Price: $10–$15
Hours: Monday–Thursday 11 a.m.–12 a.m., Friday–Saturday 11 a.m.–1 a.m., Sunday 10 a.m.–12 a.m.

Melting Pot Restaurant
125 W. Station Square Dr. Station Square
(412) 261-3477
www.meltingpot.com
Cool Features: Fondue-style dishes on a tabletop burner.

(Melting Pot, continued)
Price: $15–$35
Hours: Monday–Thursday 4 p.m.–10 p.m., Friday 4 p.m.–11 p.m., Saturday 12 p.m.–11 p.m., Sunday 12 p.m.–10 p.m.

Mighty Oak Barrel
939 Third St., Oakmont
(412) 826-1069
www.mightyoakbarrel.com
Price: $20–$30
Hours: Tuesday–Saturday 5 p.m.–10 p.m.

PD's Pub
5832 Forward Ave., Squirrel Hill
(412) 422-5027
Price: $5–$10
Cool Features: Pub classics like sandwiches and grilled dishes.
Hours: Monday–Saturday 3 p.m.–2 a.m., Sunday 4 p.m.–2 a.m.

Six Penn Kitchen
146 Sixth St., Downtown
(412) 566-7366
www.sixpennkitchen.com
Cool Features: Comfort food meets contemporary cuisine.
Price: $15–$25
Hours: Monday–Thursday 11 a.m.–11 p.m., Friday 11 a.m.–12 a.m., Saturday 3 p.m.–12 a.m., Sunday 10:30 a.m.–2:30 p.m.

Sonoma Grille

947 Penn Ave., Downtown

(412) 697-1336

www.thesonomagrille.com

Cool Features: Californian cuisine

Price: $20–$30

Hours: Daily 11 a.m.–3 p.m.,
5 p.m.–11 p.m.

Tom's Diner

1715 E. Carson St., South Side

(412) 488-0900

www.eatattomsdiner.com

Price: $8–$20

Hours: Daily 24 hours

Union Grill

413 S. Craig St., Oakland

(412) 681-8620

Price: $10–$20

Hours: Sunday–Thursday
11 a.m.–10 p.m., Friday–
Saturday 11 a.m.–11 p.m.

Other Places to Check Out:

Cheesecake Factory

Hard Rock Café

Harris Grill

Jerome Bettis' Grille 36

Jo Jo's Restaurant

Lot 17 Bar & Grill

Market Street Ale House

McFadden's Restaurant

North Park Lounge

Oakmont Tavern

Red Room

Shady Grove/Walnut Grill

FINE DINING

Capital Grille

301 Fifth Ave., Downtown

(412) 338-9100

www.thecapitalgrille.com

Price: $20–$30

Hours: Monday–Thursday
11 a.m.–3 p.m., 5 p.m.–10 p.m.,
Friday 11 a.m.–3 p.m.,
5 p.m.–11 p.m.,
Saturday 5 p.m.–11 p.m.,
Sunday 5 p.m.–10 p.m.

Grand Concourse

100 W. Station Square Dr.
Station Square

(412) 261-1717

www.muer.com

Cool Features: Located in a
beautiful, historic railroad station.

Price: $20–$40

Hours: Monday–Thursday
11 a.m.–10 p.m.,
Friday 11 a.m.–11 p.m.,
Saturday 11:30 a.m.–11 p.m.,
Sunday 3 p.m.–9 p.m.

Hyde Park Prime Steakhouse

247 North Shore Dr.
North Shore

(412) 222-4014

www.hydeparkrestaurants.com

Cool Features: $4 martini
happy hour Monday–Friday
4:30 p.m.–6:30 p.m.

Price: $20–$40

Hours: Monday–Thursday
5 p.m.–10 p.m., Friday–
Saturday 5 p.m.–11 p.m.,
Sunday 4 p.m.–9 p.m.

LeMont Restaurant

1114 Grandview, Mt. Washington

(412) 431-3100

www.lemontpittsburgh.com

Cool Features: Enjoy the view from one of Pittsburgh's most romantic restaurants.

Price: $25–$45

Hours: Monday–Saturday
5 p.m.–close,
Sunday 4 p.m.–close

McCormick & Schmick's Seafood Restaurant

301 Fifth Ave., Downtown
(412) 201-6992

2667 Sidney St., South Side
(412) 432-3260

www.mccormickandschmicks.com

Price: $20–$40

Hours: Sunday–Thursday
11 a.m.–10 p.m., Friday–
Saturday 11 a.m.–11 p.m.

Mitchell's Fish Market

185 Waterfront Dr., Homestead
(412) 476-8844

1500 Washington Rd.
Mt. Lebanon

(412) 571-3474

www.mitchellsfishmarket.com

Price: $15–$30

Hours: Monday–Thursday
11:30 a.m.–10 p.m., Friday–
Saturday 11:30 a.m.–11 p.m.,
Sunday 11:30 a.m.–9 p.m.

Monterey Bay Fish Grotto

1411 Grandview Ave.
Mt. Washington

(Monterey Bay, continued)

(412) 481-4414

146 Mall Circle Dr., Monroeville
(412) 374-8530

www.montereybayfishgrotto.com

Price: $25–$40

Hours: Monday–Thursday
11 a.m.–3 p.m., 5 p.m.–10 p.m.,
Friday–Saturday 11 a.m.–3 p.m.
(Monroeville), 5 p.m.–11 p.m.,
Sunday 5 p.m.–9 p.m.

Ruth's Chris Steak House

6 PPG Place, Downtown

(412) 391-4800

www.ruthschris.com

Price: $20–$35

Hours: Monday–Thursday
11:30 a.m.–3 p.m.,
5 p.m.–10 p.m.,
Friday 11:30 a.m.–3 p.m.,
5 p.m.–11 p.m.,
Saturday 5 p.m.–11 p.m.,
Sunday 5 p.m.–9 p.m.

Toast

5102 Baum Blvd., Shadyside

(412) 224-2579

www.toastpittsburgh.com

Price: $10–$25

Hours: Tuesday–Thursday
5 p.m.–10 p.m., Friday–
Saturday 5 p.m.–11 p.m.

Other Places to Check Out:

Georgetown Inn

Hyeholde Restaurant

Legume

Palomino Restaurant

(Other Places, continued)

Pittsburgh Chop House

Tin Angel

PIZZA

Aiello's Pizza

2112 Murray Ave., Squirrel Hill

(412) 521-9973
(412) 521-0226

www.aiellospizza.com

Price: $10–$25

Hours: Daily 11 a.m.–2 a.m.

Beto's Pizza & Restaurant

1473 Banksville Rd., Banksville

(412) 561-0121

Cool Features: The most unique pizza in town—cheese and toppings are added after the pizza comes out of the oven.

Price: $1+/slice, $8–$15 dinners

Hours: Monday–Saturday 11 a.m.–1 a.m.

Fiori's Pizzaria

103 Capital Ave., Brookline

(412) 343-7788

www.fiorispizzaria.com

Price: $10–$15

Hours: Monday–Thursday 11 a.m.–1 a.m., Friday–Saturday 11 a.m.–3 a.m., Sunday 11 a.m.–1 a.m.

Little Chicago's Pizzeria

1728 E. Carson St., South Side

(412) 431-1450

(Little Chicago's, continued)

www.littlechicago.com

Price: $8–$15

Hours: Monday–Thursday 10 a.m.–11:15 p.m., Friday–Saturday 10 a.m.–2:15 a.m., Sunday 12 p.m.–11:15 p.m.

Mineo's Pizza House

2128 Murray Ave, Squirrel Hill

(412) 521-9864

www.mineospizza.com

Cool Features: Winner of several Best Pizza awards.

Price: $10–$25

Hours: Sunday–Thursday 11 a.m.–1 a.m., Friday–Saturday 11 a.m.–2 a.m.

Napoli Pizzeria

2006 Murray Ave., Squirrel Hill

(412) 521-1744

www.napolipizzasqhill.com

Price: $5–$15

Hours: Sunday–Thursday 11 a.m.–11 p.m., Friday–Saturday 11 a.m.–12 a.m.

Pizza Sola

6004 Penn Cir. S., East Liberty
(412) 363-7652

1417 E. Carson St., South Side
(412) 481-3888

www.pizzasola.com

Price: $5–$15

Hours: Monday–Wednesday 11:30 a.m.–12 a.m., Thursday–Saturday 11:30 a.m.–3 a.m., Sunday 12:30 p.m.–12 a.m.

Other Places to Check Out:

Bella Notte

Bites 'n' Brews

Paisano's Restaurant

Pino's Mercado

Pizza Perfecta

SANDWICHES
Primanti Brothers

46 18th St., Strip District
(412) 263-2142

3803 Forbes Ave., Oakland
(412) 621-4444

1832 E. Carson St., South Side
(412) 381-2583

2 S. Market Sq., Downtown
(412) 261-1599

www.primantibrothers.com

Cool Features: Pittsburgh
sandwiches—with fries and
coleslaw on top. Easy to find
with 15 area locations.

Price: $5–$8

Hours: Strip: Daily 24 hours;
Oakland: Monday–Saturday
10 a.m.–2 a.m.,
Sunday 11 a.m.–12 a.m.;
South Side: Daily 11 a.m.–2 a.m.;
Market Square: Daily
11 a.m.–11 p.m.

Tessaro's

4601 Liberty Ave., Bloomfield
(412) 682-6809

Cool Features: Quite possibly
the best burgers in the city.

Price: $5–$10

Hours: Monday–Saturday
11 a.m.–12 a.m.

Uncle Sam's

210 Oakland Ave., Oakland
(412) 621-1885

5808 Forbes Ave., Squirrel Hill
(412) 521-7827

Cool Features: Four locations.

Price: $5–$8

Hours: Monday–Friday
10:30 a.m.–8:30 p.m.,
Saturday 11 a.m.–8 p.m.,
Sunday 11 a.m.–6 p.m.

Other Places to Check Out:

DiBella's Old Fashioned Subs

Five Guys Burgers & Fries

The Original Hot Dog Shop

Peppi's

Pretzel Shop

Red Robin

ASIAN
Bangkok Balcony

5846 Forbes Ave., Squirrel Hill
(412) 521-0728

www.bangkokbalconypgh.com

Cool Features: Excellent Thai
food in a unique atmosphere.

Price: $10–$20

Hours: Sunday–Thursday
12 p.m.–10 p.m., Friday–
Saturday 12 p.m.–11 p.m.

India Garden

328 Atwood St., Oakland
(412) 682-3000

3813 William Penn, Monroeville
(412) 372-0400

(India Garden, continued)

www.indiagarden.net

Cool Features: Lunch and dinner buffets; happy hour and late-night specials in Oakland.

Price: $10–$15

Hours: Daily 11:30 a.m.–1 a.m.

The Lemon Grass Café

124 Sixth Ave., Downtown

(412) 765-2222

Cool Features: This Thai café is a convenient stop before a show in the Cultural District.

Price: $10–$15

Hours: Monday–Thursday 11 a.m.–9 p.m., Friday–Saturday 11 a.m.–10:30 p.m., Sunday 3 p.m.–9 p.m.

Lulu's Noodles

400 S. Craig St., Oakland

(412) 687-7777

Cool Features: Easily one of the best Asian restaurants in town.

Price: $10–$15

Hours: Daily 11 a.m.–10 p.m.

Nakama Japanese Steakhouse and Sushi Bar

1611 E. Carson St., South Side

(412) 381-6000

www.eatatnakama.com

Cool Features: Hibachi chefs cook tableside.

Price: $20–$45

Hours: Monday–Saturday 11 a.m.–11 p.m., Sunday 1 p.m.–10 p.m.

Sawa

145 Mall Circle Dr., Monroeville

(412) 372-8888

Cool Features: Chefs will sometimes attempt to shoot food (and saki) into your mouth.

Price: $20–$45

Hours: Monday–Thursday 11:30 a.m.–10 p.m., Friday–Saturday 11:30 a.m.–11 p.m., Sunday 12 p.m.–10 p.m.

Sesame Inn

1 Station Sq. Dr., Station Square

(412) 281-8282

www.sesameinn.net

Cool Features: Excellent Chinese at four area locations.

Price: $10–$15

Hours: Monday–Thursday 11:30 a.m.–10 p.m., Friday–Saturday 11:30 a.m.–11 p.m., Sunday 12 p.m.–9 p.m.

Silk Elephant

1712 Murray Ave., Squirrel Hill

(412) 421-8801

www.silkelephant.net

Cool Features: Try a little of everything with some Thai tapas and an excellent wine list.

Price: $10–$20

Hours: Sunday–Thursday 11:30 a.m.–10 p.m., Friday–Saturday 11:30 a.m.–11 p.m.

Soba Lounge

5847 Ellsworth Ave., Shadyside

(412) 362-5656

Soba Lounge
www.bigburrito.com/soba
Cool Features: Pan-Asian
Price: $20–$30
Hours: Sunday–Thursday
5 p.m.–10 p.m., Friday–
Saturday 5 p.m.–11 p.m.

Sweet Basil/La Filipiniana
5321 Butler St., Lawrenceville
(412) 781-8724
2020 Murray Ave., Squirrel Hill
(412) 422-8950
www.mysweetbasil.com
Cool Features: Both Thai and
Filipino items.
Price: $10–$15
Hours: Lawrenceville – Tuesday–
Sunday 5 p.m.–10 p.m.;
Squirrel Hill – Tuesday–Friday
11:30 a.m.–3 p.m.,
5 p.m.–10 p.m., Saturday–
Sunday 12 p.m.–10 p.m.

Umi
5847 Ellsworth Ave., Shadyside
(412) 362-6198
www.bigburrito.com/umi
Cool Features: Fresh sushi!
Price: $10–$30
Hours: Tuesday–Thursday
5 p.m.–9:30 p.m., Friday–
Saturday 5 p.m.–10:30 p.m.

Other Places to Check Out:
New Dumpling House
P.F. Chang's
Pacific Rim
Richard Chen

(Other Places, continued)
Rose Tea Café
Spice Island Tea House
Taipei
Taj Mahal
Thai Place Restaurant
Tram's Kitchen
Yokoso Japanese Steak House

CARIBBEAN
Kaya
2000 Smallman St., Strip District
(412) 261-6565
www.bigburrito.com/kaya
Price: $10–$25
Hours: Monday–Wednesday
11:30 a.m.–10 p.m., Thursday–
Saturday 11:30 a.m.–11 p.m.,
Sunday 12 p.m.–9 p.m.

Other Places to Check Out:
Bahama Breeze
Seviche

ETHIOPIAN
Abay Ethiopian Cuisine
130 S. Highland Ave., Shadyside
(412) 661-9736
www.abayrestaurant.com
Price: $15–$20
Hours: Tuesday–Saturday
11:30 a.m.–2:30 p.m.,
5 p.m.–10 p.m.,
Sunday 11:30 a.m.–2:30 p.m.,
5 p.m.–9 p.m.

Tana Ethiopian Cuisine
5929 Baum Blvd., East Liberty
(412) 665-2770
www.tanaethiopancuisine.com
Price: $8–$15
Hours: Monday 5 p.m.–11 p.m.,
Tuesday–Sunday
11 a.m.–2:30 p.m.,
5 p.m.–11 p.m.

ITALIAN
Café Allegro
51 S. 12th St., South Side
(412) 481-7788
www.cafeallegropittsburgh.com
Price: $20–$30
Hours: Sunday–Thursday
5 p.m.–10 p.m., Friday–
Saturday 5 p.m.–11 p.m.

D'Amico's
4744 Liberty Ave., Bloomfield
(412) 682-2523
Price: $15–$30
Hours: Daily 11 a.m.–11 p.m.

Dish Osteria Bar
127 S. 17th St., South Side
(412) 390-2012
www.dishosteria.com
Price: $15–$30
Hours: Monday–Saturday
5 p.m.–2 a.m.

Girasole
733 Copeland St., Shadyside
(412) 682-2130
www.733copeland.com
Cool Features: Seasonal menu.
Price: $10–$20
Hours: Tuesday–Thursday
11:30 a.m.–10 p.m., Friday–
Saturday 11:30 a.m.–11 p.m.,
Sunday 4 p.m.–9 p.m.

Il Pizzaiolo
703 Washington Rd.
Mt. Lebanon
(412) 344-4123
Cool Features: Authentic Italian
pastas and wood-fired pizzas.
Price: $15–$25
Hours: Monday–Thursday
12 p.m.–10 p.m., Friday–
Saturday 12 p.m.–11 p.m.,
Sunday 12 p.m.–9 p.m.

Joe Mama's Italian Deluxe
3716 Forbes Ave., Oakland
(412) 621-7282
www.joemamas.com
Price: $10–$15
Hours: Daily 11 a.m.–12 a.m.

Lidia's Pittsburgh Pasta
1400 Smallman St., Strip District
(412) 552-0150
www.lidias-pittsburgh.com
Cool Features: One of just
two Lidia Bastianich eateries
outside of New York City.
Price: $15–$30

(Lidia's, continued)

Hours: Monday–Thursday
11:30 a.m.–2 p.m., 5 p.m.–9 p.m.,
Friday 5 p.m.–10 p.m.,
Saturday 11 a.m.–2:30 p.m.,
5 p.m.–10 p.m.,
Sunday 5 p.m.–8 p.m.

Pizzutti's

709 Bellefonte St., Shadyside
(412) 687-1022
Price: $10–$25
Hours: Monday–Thursday
11 a.m.–2 p.m., 5 p.m.–9 p.m.,
Friday–Saturday 11 a.m.–2 p.m.,
5 p.m.–10 p.m.

Other Places to Check Out:

Alexander's Pasta Express
Bruschetta's
Café Roma
Franco's Trattoria
Joseph Tambellini Restaurant
La Tavola
Piccolo Forno
Zarra's

MEDITERRANEAN

Casbah

229 S. Highland Ave., Shadyside
(412) 661-5656
www.bigburrito.com/casbah
Price: $15–$30
Hours: Monday–Thursday
11:30 a.m.–2:30 p.m.,
5 p.m.–10 p.m.,
Friday 11:30 a.m.–2:30 p.m.,
5 p.m.–11 p.m.,

(Casbah, continued)

Saturday 5 p.m.–11 p.m.,
Sunday 11 a.m.–2 p.m.,
5 p.m.–9 p.m.

Gypsy Café

1330 Bingham St., South Side
(412) 381-4977
www.gypsycafe.net
Price: $10–$20
Hours: Wednesday
5 p.m.–10 p.m., Thursday–
Saturday 5 p.m.–11 p.m.,
Sunday 12 p.m.–9 p.m.

Le Pommier

2104 E. Carson St., South Side
(412) 431-1901
www.lepommier.com
Cool Features: French bistro
Price: $20–$40
Hours: Monday–Thursday
5:30 p.m.–9:30 p.m., Friday–
Saturday 5 p.m.–close

Tusca

2773 Sidney St., South Side
(412) 488-9000
www.tuscatapas.com
Cool Features: Tapas from
Greece, Italy, Spain, the Middle
East, and Morocco
Price: $5–$14
Hours: Sunday–Monday
12 p.m.–8 p.m.,
Tuesday 11 a.m.–10 p.m.,
Wednesday–Thursday
11 a.m.–11 p.m., Friday–
Saturday 11 a.m.–12 a.m.

Other Places to Check Out:

Reynold's on Bryant Restaurant

Aladdin's Eatery

Mike & Tony's Gyros

MEXICAN

Azul Bar y Cantina

122 Broad St., Leetsdale

(724) 266-6362

www.azulbarycantina.com

Price: $8–$15

Hours: Monday–Thursday
11 a.m.–9 p.m., Friday–
Saturday 11 a.m.–11 p.m.

El Campesino

4771 McKnight Rd., North Hills
(412) 366-8730

4063 William Penn, Monroeville
(412) 787-2225

www.elcampesino.net

Cool Features: Authentic
Mexican, four area locations

Price: $10–$15

Hours: Monday–Thursday
11:30 a.m.–10 p.m.,
Friday 11:30 a.m.–10:30 p.m.,
Saturday 12 p.m.–10:30 p.m.,
Sunday 12 p.m.–9 p.m.

Mad Mex

20510 Perry Hwy., Cranberry
(724) 741-5656

4100 William Penn, Monroeville
(412) 349-6767

7905 McKnight Rd., North Hills
(412) 366-5656

(Mad Mex, continued)

370 Atwood St., Oakland
(412) 681-5656

2 Robinson Plaza, Robinson Twp.
(412) 494-5656

2101 Greentree Rd., South Hills
(412) 279-0200

madmex.com

Cool Features: Hilarious menu;
late-night hours and half-price
specials at select locations.

Price: $8–$15

Hours: Monday–Thursday
11 a.m.–11 p.m., Friday–
Saturday 11 a.m.–12 a.m.,
Sunday 11 a.m.–10 p.m.

SPANISH

Ibiza Tapas & Wine Bar

2224 E. Carson St., South Side

(412) 325-2227

www.ibizatapasrestaurant.com

Cool Features: Tapas and wines
from around the world.

Price: $10–$30

Hours: Monday–Thursday
4 p.m.–12 a.m., Friday–
Saturday 4 p.m.–1 a.m.

La Casa

5884 Ellsworth Ave., Shadyside

(412) 441-3090

www.casablanca212.com

Cool Features: Spanish tapas

Price: $10–$25

Hours: Sunday–Friday
4:30 p.m.–close,
Saturday 11:30 a.m.–close

Mallorca

2228 E. Carson St., South Side

(412) 488-1818

www.mallorcarestaurant.com

Price: $15–$35

Hours: Monday–Thursday
11:30 a.m.–10:30 p.m., Friday–
Saturday 11:30 a.m.–11:30 p.m.,
Sunday 12 p.m.–10 p.m.

SWEETS & BAKED GOODS

Dave & Andy's Homemade Ice Cream

207 Atwood St., Oakland

(412) 681-9906

Cool Features: 25-plus flavors
of ice cream and frozen yogurt.

Price: $2–$8

Hours: Monday–Friday
11:30 a.m.–10 p.m., Saturday–
Sunday 12 p.m.–10 p.m.

Moio's Italian Pastry Shop

4209 William Penn, Monroeville

(412) 372-6700

www.moios.com

Price: $5 and up

Hours: Tuesday–Saturday
9 a.m.–7:30 p.m.,
Sunday 9 a.m.–5 p.m.

Oakmont Bakery

531 Allegheny Ave., Oakmont

(412) 826-1606

www.oakmontbakery.com

Price: Varies by purchase

(Oakmont Bakery, continued)

Hours: Monday–Saturday
6 a.m.–7 p.m.,
Sunday 6 a.m.–3 p.m.

Oh Yeah!

232 S. Highland Ave., Shadyside

(412) 253-0955

www.customswirl.com

Cool Features: More than 100
"swirl in" ice cream toppings,
plus coffee, waffles, and more!

Price: $5–$15

Hours: Monday–Thursday
7 a.m.–10 p.m., Friday–
Saturday 7 a.m.–2 a.m.,
Sunday 9 a.m.–10 p.m.

Prantl's Bakery

5525 Walnut St., Shadyside

(412) 621-2092

www.shop.prantlsbakery.com

Cool Features: Famous for their
burnt almond torte.

Price: Varies by purchase.

Hours: Tuesday–Saturday
7:30 a.m.–6 p.m.,
Sunday 9 a.m.–1 p.m.

Other Places to Check Out:

Coco's Cupcake Café

Dozen Bake Shop

Enrico Biscotti Co.

Klavon's Authentic Ice Cream

Mancini's Bakery

Mon Aimee Chocolat

Mulberry Street Creamery

Paddy Cake

Vanilla Pastry Studio

Best Bakery:
Oakmont Bakery
Prantl's Bakery

Best Breakfast:
Pamela's
Square Café

Best Burger:
Fat Heads Saloon
Tessaro's

Best Chinese:
Lulu's Noodles
Sesame Inn

Best Coffee:
Beehive Coffee Shop
La Prima Espresso Co.

Best Desserts:
Gullifty's Restaurant

Best Ice Cream:
Dave & Andy's Homemade
Ice Cream
Oh Yeah!

Best Indian:
India Garden

Best Italian:
Dish
Girasole
Lidia's Pittsburgh Pasta

Best Mexican:
Azul Bar y Cantina
El Campesino
Mad Mex

Best Pizza:
Il Pizzaiolo
Mineo's Pizza House

Best Sandwiches:
Primanti Brothers

Best Seafood:
McCormick & Schmick's
Monterey Bay Fish Grotto

Best Sushi:
Nakama Japanese Steakhouse
Umi

Best Thai:
Bangkok Balcony
Lemon Grass Café

Best Vegetarian:
Kaya
The Quiet Storm
Zenith

Best Wine List:
Mallorca

Best Wings:
Fat Heads Saloon

→

Best Fine Dining:
LeMont Restaurant

Monterey Bay Fish Grotto

Best Outdoor Dining:
Double Wide Grill

Mallorca

Best Place to Take a Date:
Ibiza

Mt. Washington restaurants

Soba

Best Place to Take a Business Client:
Capital Grille

Eleven

Nakama

Best View:
Anything on Grandview Avenue in Mt. Washington

Best Late-Night Meal:
Fuel & Fuddle

India Garden

Best 24-Hour Dining:
Eat'n Park

Primanti Bros.

Tom's Diner

Grocery Stores:
East End Food Co-op

7516 Meade St., East End
(412) 242-3598

www.eastendfoodcoop.com

Giant Eagle

More than 50 locations across the city. Offers 10-cent discounts on fuel for every $50 spent in-store.

www.gianteagle.com

Trader Joe's

6343 Penn Ave., East Liberty
(412) 363-5748

www.traderjoes.com

Whole Foods Market

5880 Centre Ave., East Liberty
(412) 441-7960

www.wholefoodsmarket.com

Wholesale Markets:
Pennsylvania Macaroni Co.

2010 Penn Ave., Strip District
(412) 471-8330

www.pennmac.com

Wholesale Produce Industry

2100 Smallman St., Strip District
(412) 391-8711

Wholey's Fish Market

1501 Penn Ave., Strip District
(412) 391-3737

www.wholey.com

Did You Know?

Pittsburgh Food Firsts

- The banana split was invented in 1904 by David Strickler, then **a pharmacist's assistant at Tassel Pharmacy in Latrobe**.

- Jim Delligatti **created the Big Mac in 1967** at his McDonald's restaurant in Uniontown. After being tested in three other area restaurants, the Big Mac became a staple of McDonald's menus nationwide.

- David L. Clark founded the D.L. Clark Company in 1886 in Pittsburgh's North Side. Clark's most famous creations were **the Clark candy bar, now produced by Necco**, and the Zagnut candy bar, now produced by Hershey.

- Ever heard of a Turkey Devonshire? This delicious gem was created in **Pittsburgh's Oakland neighborhood in 1936** and features turkey or chicken served baked in an open-faced sandwich with bacon, cream sauce, and cheese.

- The H.J. Heinz Company was founded in 1869 in Sharpsburg. In 1876, the company introduced what would become its most famous product—**Heinz Ketchup, the only acceptable ketchup** for any self-respecting Pittsburgher.

- Italian wedding soup, **served at most Pittsburgh-area restaurants and at many local wedding receptions**, consists of a chicken-based broth, small meatballs, tiny bead-like pasta, and spinach or escarole.

- Isaly's, a chain of dairies and restaurants originally founded in central Ohio, is one of Pittsburgh's adopted originals. Its **famous Klondike bars, skyscraper ice cream cones, and chipped ham**—made from razor-thin slices of chopped ham—hold a special place in the hearts of the locals.

- The "almost famous" Primanti Brothers sandwiches are a Pittsburgh institution that consist of a grilled meat of your choice, cheese, tomato, **a vinegar-based coleslaw, and French fries** between two slices of Italian bread.

- In this city, nearly all entrée-size salads come with the fried goodies, and **once you've had a taste, those other salads seem bland** and boring by comparison.

Locals Speak Out On...
City Dining

> "Sandwiches from Primanti Bros.—famous for including fries and coleslaw between the bread instead of on the side—are a Pittsburgh standby, but for good reason: These sandwiches are absolutely awesome!"

Q "I am a huge fan of breakfast food, and the Square Café in Regent Square is definitely my favorite place to go for breakfast. They have a lot of unique items, ranging from **pumpkin pancakes to a delicious breakfast quesadilla**. The restaurant also has a really great atmosphere: It is decorated in funky square patterns and features work by local artists. And last but certainly not least, the Square Café makes a great cup of coffee or latte."

Q "Casbah has the best pork chop in town. They serve an amazing brunch at Six Penn Kitchen, **plus it has a great atmosphere and a rooftop deck**. Seviche has a great vibe, and Mineo's Pizza is the best pizza I have ever tasted."

Q "The Double Wide Grill has a fun, unique atmosphere with some outdoor seating, a large bar, and **a creative menu that never disappoints with deliciousness**. Harris Grill in Shadyside also has a balance of outdoor and indoor seating with great drink specials and a menu that nobody can duplicate."

Q "Lidia's in the Strip has three excellent pasta choices made fresh daily, and it has a great atmosphere. Kaya, also in the Strip, has **an incredible array of authentic Caribbean/Pacific food and drinks**, and they often feature local produce in their recipes. You have to try the black bean dip, but everything is great."

Q "Mallorca has great Spanish cuisine and sangria. Alexander's Pasta Express has **good Italian food and cheap-but-yummy create-your-own pasta dishes**."

Q "The Oakmont Tavern has a good atmosphere and good food. The Mighty Oak Barrel is **an intimate restaurant with unique menu items**. Mad Mex is a great Mexican restaurant with good happy hour specials."

Q "Girasole is a great family-owned restaurant in Shadyside. The atmosphere is very quaint, and the Italian food is authentic and delicious. Also, Walnut Grill is **a great local place with bordering-on-gourmet food**. It is very trendy, and the clientele is fairly young. Their seared tuna is highly recommended."

Q "**Toast is a new place with great service**! Paul Tebbets and Chef Chet are very hospitable and care about the dining experience for their customers!"

Q "Six Penn Kitchen in the Cultural District downtown has great food at a great value. **With a seasonal, interesting menu that really focuses on local products**, it's a great place to eat before a show. Legume in Regent Square is a great little BYOB with a small menu that changes daily. The food is fantastic, and it's a very warm, hospitable place. Eleven in the Strip District is always fantastic and has a nice bar area with a lounge menu."

Q "Asian food is my absolute favorite, and I would recommend Lulu's Noodles in Oakland to anyone who shares this sentiment. I have never ordered something from Lulu's that I didn't like, and their menu offers a wide variety of both noodle and rice dishes. The restaurant is also known for its delicious bubble teas and smoothies made on-site from fresh fruit. **Lulu's is hugely popular among both college students and professionals**, and while it always seems fairly busy, customers are usually seated right away or within a few minutes of arriving."

Q "Oh man, there are too many restaurants to recommend. **The Indian food here is unmatched**! There are so many good ones, but India Garden is our favorite. Richard Chen just opened a restaurant here—he has the only Chinese restaurant in Vegas with a Michelin star. Quiet Storm is a great vegan/vegetarian café, and Red Room has a chef that specializes in molecular gastronomy. Eleven has the best ruffled potato chips ever. The Strip District is a great place to get specialty foods like cheese or seafood at wholesale prices."

Q "Tessaro's has awesome burgers. **Fat Heads has a great bar and burgers**, and DeLuca's is just greasy and awesome."

Q "Pamela's in the Strip is great for breakfast. Plan to stand in line on a Sunday morning, but it's worth it. You can actually **feel your arteries hardening just by ordering the Lounge fries** at North Park Lounge on Babcock, but it'd be a delicious way to go. Try DiBella Subs in Robinson—I could eat their homemade oil dressing on ice cream. Church Brew Works is another restaurant with great food, great beer, and a unique setting...unless you're used to drinking in church."

Q "Business clients and dates alike would absolutely love Six Penn Kitchen. **Not only is the food unreal, but the atmosphere is perfect for conversation**."

Q "Le Pommier is a French bistro on the South Side with a casual elegance and great French food. The 17th Street Café is a great neighborhood restaurant. Piccolo Forno is **a good inexpensive Italian restaurant that is hip without trying too hard**."

Q "**Pamela's is a great breakfast/brunch place for a weekend get-together**. Uncle Sam's has great steak subs and fries. Fuel and Fuddle is great for half-price late-night food, along with Joe Mama's. PD's Pub has some very tasty 30-cent wings on select days."

Q "The Melting Pot, Yokoso, Chop House, and Ruth's Chris **all have wonderful steak and nice atmospheres.**"

Q "Bangkok Balcony, a Thai restaurant in Squirrel Hill, is a great place to take a date. The dining area is on the upper floor of the building, and customers who sit by the window get **a great view of Squirrel Hill's charming shopping district**. The food is delicious yet affordable, and while the atmosphere is hip and fun, the restaurant isn't so loud or busy as to impede conversation. Also, Bangkok Balcony is located near a movie theater, a bowling alley, and several coffee shops—just in case you need somewhere else to take that date!"

Q "Pittsburgh has a surprising number of Spanish restaurants focusing on tapas, such as Ibiza, La Casa, Tusca, and Mallorca, and each one is fantastic. Also, **Primanti Brothers is the signature Pittsburgh sandwich**, where the fries and coleslaw are put directly on the sandwich instead on the side. It's messy, but it always delivers."

Q "Palomino is very good for dinner but also **has a nice late-night bar menu for after a show or game**. I like La Tavola in Mt. Washington for Italian, and Ibiza is nice for tapas."

Q "PD's Pub in Squirrel Hill is a very low-key bar with very good food and drinks. **Fuel and Fuddle in Oakland has awesome half-price specials at night**. Pamela's is everywhere, and they have a great breakfast."

Q "I randomly found the Gypsy Café in the South Side when it first opened. I've been going there ever since, and now reservations are almost necessary. **The place is quaint and intimate, and the menu is always delicious**. They change it seasonally, so it forces you to try new dishes."

Q "The Pittsburgh steak (or chicken) salad is the best. Putting **French fries on top of a salad is genius**. It always amazes me now when a salad does not come with fries."

The Urban Guru Take On...
City Dining

When the average person thinks of Pittsburgh, world-class cuisine probably doesn't jump to mind—but that's exactly what you'll find. Fortunately for food lovers, Pittsburgh's culinary diversity is much richer than its ethnic diversity. You'll find food representative of nearly every region of the world, and there are many outstanding establishments serving a variety of American cuisine, from staples like pizza and burgers to unique vegetarian meals and modern fusion dishes. Dining options are similarly diverse in atmosphere, style, and price, with many new chefs planning menus around local produce and changing offerings seasonally—keeping things "fresh" on several levels. Best of all, Pittsburgh has many restaurants taking a contemporary approach to traditional cuisine, leaving hungry locals with an endless variety of new and delicious creations to try.

Because many of Pittsburgh's best dining districts are the same as its best shopping and entertainment districts, it's easy to find a great meal to fit any itinerary. Neighborhoods like Oakland, Shadyside, Squirrel Hill, the South Side, and the Strip District are packed with a range of eateries for any mood, taste, occasion, or budget. Great restaurants are found throughout the city, though, so all you need to find Pittsburgh's best is transportation and an open mind.

The Urban Guru® Grade on

City Dining: A-

A high City Dining grade implies that restaurants are affordable, accessible, and worth visiting. Other factors include the variety of cuisine and the availability of alternative options (vegetarian, vegan, kosher).

Nightlife

The Lowdown On...
Nightlife

Club and Bar Prowler: Popular Nightlife Spots!

BLOOMFIELD/ LAWRENCEVILLE

Belvedere's
4016 Butler St.
(412) 687-2555
Music-friendly local bar with variety of patrons, punk rock shows, and pool tables.

Bloomfield Bridge Tavern
4412 Liberty Ave.
(412) 682-8611
www.myspace.com/ polishpartyhouse
The Bloomfield Bridge Tavern (BBT) is a popular bar known for its live music, drum and bass nights, drink specials, and variety of delicious Polish food.

Brillobox
4104 Penn Ave.
(412) 621-4900

➡

(Brillobox, continued)

brillobox.net

The Brillobox is a popular swanky lounge that draws a loyal hipster crowd with live bands, theme nights, and a vegetarian menu.

The Church Brew Works

3525 Liberty Ave.

(412) 688-8200

www.churchbrew.com

This former St. John the Baptist church serves up an extensive selection of hand-crafted beers.

DOWNTOWN

Bossa Nova

123 7th Ave.

(412) 232-3030

www.bossanovapgh.com

Bossa Nova serves up global tapas, cocktails, and martinis in a cozy atmosphere.

Olive or Twist

140 Sixth St.

(412) 255-0525

www.olive-twist.com

Located next to Heinz Hall, Olive or Twist is Pittsburgh's premier martini bar.

Pegasus Lounge

818 Liberty Ave.

(412) 281-2131

www.pittpegasus.com

(Pegasus, continued)

Pittsburgh's premier gay/lesbian nightclub features contests, drink specials, and theme nights.

Seviche

930 Penn Ave.

(412) 697-3120

www.seviche.com

Offering happy hour specials and Nuevo Latino tapas, Seviche is a hot spot downtown.

EAST LIBERTY

Kelly's Bar & Lounge

6012 Penn Circle South

(412) 363-6012

Restored 40s-era bar offers 12 taps of imported and craft-brewed beer and a hip crowd.

Red Room Café/2Red Lounge

134 S. Highland Ave.

(412) 362-5800

www.redroomcafe.net

Increasingly popular with the young professional crowd, Red Room offers a swanky intimate atmosphere.

Sharp Edge Beer Emporium

302 S. St. Clair St.

(412) 661-3537

www.sharpedgebeer.com

Just steps from Baum Boulevard, the Sharp Edge has an extensive list of beers, particularly Belgian drafts.

NORTH SIDE

Calico Jack's Cantina

353 N. Shore Dr.

(412) 322-7380

www.calicojackspitt.com

Close to both stadiums, CJ's combines drink specials, a lively atmosphere, and the motto "Everything Goes at Calicos."

McFadden's Restaurant and Saloon

211 N. Shore Dr.

(412) 322-3470

www.mcfaddenspitt.com

Located next to PNC Park, McFadden's offers drink specials, theme nights, 30 HD flat screens, a huge dance floor, and a full menu.

Penn Brewery

800 Vinial St.

(412) 237-9400

www.pennbrew.com

Sample microbrews from this authentic German brewery.

OAKLAND

Fuel & Fuddle

212 Oakland Ave.

(412) 682-3473

www.fuelandfuddle.com

Fuel & Fuddle has an impressive list of beers and an even better menu. Check out the late-night food discounts.

Hemingway's Café

3911 Forbes Ave.

(412) 621-4100

www.hemingways-cafe.com

A popular bar in the heart of Oakland, Hemingway's is known for its unbeatable daily draft specials and lively atmosphere.

Mad Mex

370 Atwood St.

(412) 681-5656

www.madmex.com

Mad Mex is the place for happy hour with its creative margaritas, half-price wings and drafts, and amazing Cal-Mex fare.

SHADYSIDE

Alto Lounge

728 Copeland St.

(412) 682-1076

www.altolounge.com

Located above the Pittsburgh Deli Company, Alto Lounge features over a dozen different types of specialty martinis.

Bites and Brews

5750 Ellsworth Ave.

(412) 361-4425

www.b2restaurants.com/ bitesandbrews

With incredible pizza and an extensive selection of beer, Bites and Brews is a prime happy hour destination.

Buffalo Blues
216 S. Highland Ave.
(412) 362-5837
www.b2restaurants.com/buffaloblues
Sample any of Buffalo Blues' 30 beers on tap while sitting at its huge U-shaped bar or extensive restaurant seating.

Harris Grill
5747 Ellsworth Ave.
(412) 362-5273
www.harrisgrill.com
Offering great outdoor seating, the Harris Grill features half-price drafts, frozen cosmos, and wings during the week for happy hour.

Le Mardi Gras
731 Copeland St.
(412) 683-0912
www.lemardigras.com
A favorite destination in Shady Side for those looking for a strong drink.

Shady Grove/Walnut Grill
5500 Walnut St.
(412) 697-0909
www.eatwalnut.com
With Shady Grove located on the first floor and Walnut Grill just a flight away, patrons have the choice of visiting two separate bars at one address, both with great food and drink options.

William Penn Tavern
739 Bellefonte St.
(412) 621-1000
www.williampenntavern.net
The William Penn Tavern, Shadyside's own sports tavern, offers daily drink specials.

SOUTH SIDE
Carson City Saloon
1401 E. Carson St.
(412) 481-3203
www.carsoncitysaloon.com
What was once a bank is now one of the most popular bars in the South Side, with TVs at each table and beer pong.

Casey's Draft House
1811 E. Carson St.
(412) 431-3595
Casey's is a popular stop on any bar crawl with arguably one of the best outdoor decks in the South Side.

Dee's Café
1316 E. Carson St.
(412) 431-1314
www.deescafe.com
A locals' favorite, Dee's Café epitomizes a neighborhood bar, with cheap drinks, pool tables, jukeboxes, and loyal regulars.

Diesel Club Lounge
1601 E. Carson St.
(412) 431-8800

(Diesel, continued)

www.dieselpgh.com

With live entertainment five nights a week, multi-level Diesel draws in huge crowds for concerts and DJs.

The Dolce Lounge

2829 E. Carson St.

(412) 586-7422

www.thedolcelounge.com

Located at the SouthSide Works, Dolce is an upscale lounge with Italian cuisine and VIP bottle service.

Double Wide Grill

2339 E. Carson St.

(412) 390-1111

doublewidegrill.com

A unique change of pace from the typical South Side bars, the Double Wide has extensive outdoor seating.

Elixir Ultra Lounge

1500 E. Carson St.

(412) 481-1811

www.elixirpgh.com

This two-story lounge offers a swanky alternative to other South Side bars with bottle service and an upstairs dance floor.

Fat Heads Saloon

1805 E. Carson St.

(412) 431-7433

www.fatheads.com

(Fat Heads, continued)

A local favorite, Fat Heads has one of the best beer lists and menus in the city—a must for anyone visiting the South Side.

Lava Lounge

2204 E. Carson St.

(412) 431-5282

www.lavaloungepgh.com

One of Pittsburgh's most original and interesting bars— you have to experience its unique atmosphere for yourself.

The Library

2304 E. Carson St.

(412) 381-0517

www.thelibrary-pgh.com

With menus located inside books and choices like Edgar Allen Potatoes, The Library stays true to its namesake, and its upstairs deck is one of the South Side's nicest outdoor options.

Mario's

1514 E. Carson St.

(412) 381-5610

www.mariospgh.com

One of the South Side's best bars, Mario's is ultimately two bars combined into one.

Nakama Japanese Steakhouse and Sushi Bar

1611 E. Carson St.

(412) 381-6000

www.eatatnakama.com

(Nakama, continued)

Nakama is the place for a good drink and friendly crowd, especially at happy hour.

Piper's Pub

1828 E. Carson St.

(412) 381-3977

www.piperspub.com

Offering an incredible selection of draft and import beers, Piper's is the place to go for an authentic pub atmosphere.

S Bar

1713 E. Carson St.

(412) 481-7227

www.sbarpgh.com

S Bar combines a posh lounge with an upscale night club in a convenient South Side location.

Tiki Lounge

2003 E. Carson St.

(412) 381-8454

www.tikilounge.biz

Experience the recreation of 1960s high-style tiki bars right on East Carson Street.

The Town Tavern

2009 E. Carson St.

(412) 325-8696

www.towntavernpittsburgh.com

One of the South Side's largest dance clubs, The Town Tavern has nightly specials and events.

Z Lounge

2108 E. Carson St.

(412) 431-1800

www.zloungepgh.com

Home to one of Pittsburgh's best bartenders, Z Lounge offers a great atmosphere and DJs spinning everything but Top 40.

STATION SQUARE

Bar Louie

240 Station Square Dr.

(412) 394-0500

www.BarLouieAmerica.com

Enjoy a hand-crafted specialty cocktail or a variety of beers and wines at this contemporary bar/restaurant in Station Square.

Barroom Pittsburgh

Station Square Dr.

(412) 434-4850

www.barroompittsburgh.com

A new addition to Station Square, the Barroom offers patrons a huge dance floor, outdoor seating, and multiple bars—all in a VIP atmosphere.

Buckhead Saloon

225 Station Square Dr.

(412) 232-3101

www.buckheadpittsburgh.com

From DJ dance parties to live bands, Buckhead Saloon is a popular destination for those ready to party in Pittsburgh.

The Funny Bone
242 W. Station Square Dr.
(412) 281-3130
www.funnybonepgh.com
Bringing in top comedians, the Funny Bone is one of Pittsburgh's best comedy clubs.

Hard Rock Café
230 W. Station Square Dr.
(412) 481-ROCK
www.hardrock.com
The Pittsburgh Hard Rock showcases both national and local bands.

Matrix
7 E. Station Square Dr.
(412) 261-2220
www.matrixpgh.com
Four nightclubs and nine bars under one roof. Beware: Thursdays are college nights.

Zen Social Club
125 W. Station Square Dr.
(412) 918-1637
www.zensocialclub.com
This luxurious multi-level nightclub offers DJs, bottle service, and private VIP lounge in an Eastern atmosphere.

STRIP DISTRICT
Altar Bar
1620 Penn Ave.
(412) 263-2877
www.thealtarbar.com
Altar Bar in the Strip hosts a variety of events from live bands to Latin Thursdays.

Firehouse Lounge
2216 Penn Ave.
(412) 434-1230
www.firehouse-lounge.com
This former firehouse is a popular nightlife destinations for the young and hip crowd.

Privilége Ultralounge
1650 Smallman St.
(412) 253-7330
www.privilegepgh.com
Privilége is a premier night spot in the Strip that can accommodate 1,100 guests.

Roland's Seafood Grill
1904 Penn Ave.
(412) 261-3401
www.rolandsseafoodgrill.com
A 50-year staple in the Strip, Roland's has an assortment of imports and domestics to enjoy.

Useful Resources for Nightlife
pitt2night.com
www.heypittsburgh.com

Locals' Favorites:
Fat Heads Saloon
Firehouse Lounge
Mad Mex

Best Atmosphere:
Elixir
Firehouse Lounge
Red Room

Best Beer Selection:
Fat Heads Saloon
Sharp Edge Beer Emporium

Best Dancing:
Diesel
Firehouse Lounge
Matrix

Best Happy Hour:
Mad Mex
Nakama
Olive or Twist

Cheapest Place to Get a Drink:
Dee's Café
Mario's

Other Places to Check Out:
Archie's
Goosky's
Redbeard's Mountain Resort & Yacht Club
The Smiling Moose
Zen Social Club

Primary Areas with Nightlife:
Shadyside
South Side
Station Square
The Strip District

Bars Close at:
2 a.m.

Gambling Options

Development for a new casino in Pittsburgh is underway on the North Shore. The $780 million facility is scheduled to open in August 2009 and will feature 3,000 slot machines, five restaurants, several lounges, and an amphitheater. Around Pittsburgh, there are various gambling options available. The Meadows Racetrack and Casino in Washington, Pa., offers horse racing and slot machines. Those looking for table games can cross the border and head to Wheeling Island or the Mountaineer Casino in West Virginia.

Locals Speak Out On...
Nightlife

"There is a variety of nightlife. Oakland and South Side are full of more low-key dive bars for catching up with friends or watching a game. Station Square or the Strip have more high-class establishments as well as dance clubs."

Q "**Pittsburgh is broken up into a couple different areas**: Station Square, which has a few different club-type places, the Strip District, which has some bars and a couple nice clubs, and the South Side, which has a little bit for everyone—dive bars, sports bars, and clubs."

Q "It totally depends on what you like. **There is something for everyone** from huge clubs with massive numbers of cookie-cutter people and generic music to dive bars with local music and everything in between."

Q "The nearby casino and gambling options are downright awful. **Save your money and go to Vegas**."

Q "The nightlife is decent. You can always find people out on Thursdays, Fridays, and Saturdays. **Going out all the other days of the week is acceptable** also. It's also less crowded, which is a plus! Where are the best bars located? I would say South Side—there is just a large variety, and they are all close together, which makes it nice."

Q "The nightlife is very oriented toward college and 20-somethings. **South Side has the best selection, but the crowd is getting out of hand**. I love hanging out downtown on a Friday after work."

Q "**The nightlife is crazy**. People are rowdy and out to get wasted. The South Side is one big bar crawl. The Strip District is all clubs, and Station Square is mostly clubs."

Q "The South Side and the Strip are good nightlife spots because **there are tons of bars and clubs clumped together**."

Q "**The nightlife is hit or miss**. The best bars are located in Shadyside or South Side."

Q "The best bars are located in the South Side. I recommend S Bar and Nakama. Nearby, **the only gambling options right now are in West Virginia**."

Q "Go to the South Side—**it's bar, club, and music central**."

Q "I love the Double Wide Grill for just sitting outside and relaxing and Nakama for happy hour. **The Strip District is full of bars and clubs**."

Q "**Nightlife in this city is ridiculous**. People get drunk, drive drunk, and walk (stumble) around making fun of people that don't look like them. Everyone wants to be so sophisticated, but this isn't New York."

Q "Nightlife is mainly the South Side, but **I prefer the bars in the suburbs**."

Q "South Side! **You can find any type of bar imaginable on East Carson Street**."

Q "It depends on what you are looking for. Shadyside has a more upscale young professional scene. Squirrel Hill is more relaxed with **a neighborhood feel and actual diversity of patrons**. If you want to get wasted and party until 2 a.m., hit the South Side. For larger clubs, try the Strip District or Station Square."

The Urban Guru Take On...
Nightlife

Pittsburgh's nightlife can be summed up in three words: lively, diverse, and abundant. There truly is never a shortage of things to do in the city. With an excess of bars, nightclubs, hookah lounges, comedy clubs, live music venues, gallery crawls, and sporting events, Pittsburgh is a vibrant city with nightlife options for any crowd. With so many different neighborhoods, it's only appropriate that each cater to different scenes.

The most active nightlife areas in the city include the South Side, Station Square, Strip District, and Shadyside. East Carson Street in the South Side, renowned for its extensive options of bars, is a one-stop destination for hole-in-the-wall bars, dance clubs, sports bars, hookah bars, and live music. The Pennsylvania Tourism Office states that East Carson Street has "more bars per capita than almost any other place on earth." Across the city, there has been a rise of swanky ultralounges. These chic clubs with dress codes, dancing, and bottle service—mainly located in the South Side and Strip—make respectable attempts to replicate those in New York and L.A. What's great about Pittsburgh is that a few doors down from some of these ultralounges are modest, local bars that have been established for generations. The eclectic mix of nightlife in Pittsburgh brings a variety of options to every bar goer.

The Urban Guru® Grade on
Nightlife: A-

A high grade in Nightlife indicates that there are many bars and clubs in the area that are easily accessible and affordable. Other determining factors include the atmosphere of the bars, drink specials, and covers.

Arts & Entertainment

The Lowdown On...
Arts & Entertainment

Galleries, Museums, & Cultural Attractions:

Pittsburgh is ranked as one of the best mid-sized cities for the arts—and for good reason. The Cultural District is filled with galleries and theaters, and there are first-class museums and attractions throughout the city and region.

Andy Warhol Museum

117 Sandusky St., North Shore
(412) 237-8300

(Warhol Museum, continued)

www.warhol.org

Hours: Tuesday–Sunday
10 a.m.–5 p.m.

The world's largest single-artist museum, it contains more than 4,000 of Warhol's original works.

August Wilson Center for African American Culture

Liberty Avenue at 10th Street, Downtown

(412) 258-2700

www.africanculture.org

(Wilson Center, continued)

Opening in Spring 2009, this all-new center features galleries, classrooms, and performing arts spaces dedicated to African American culture.

Carnegie Museums of Art and Natural History

4400 Forbes Ave., Oakland

(412) 622-3131

www.cmoa.org
www.carnegiemnh.org

Hours: Tuesday–Saturday 10 a.m.–5 p.m. (8 p.m. Thursday), Sunday 12 p.m.–5 p.m.

Two renowned museums sit side by side in a complex that also houses the Carnegie Library.

Carnegie Science Center

1 Allegheny Ave., North Shore

(412) 237-3400

www.carnegiesciencecenter.org

Hours: Sunday–Friday 10 a.m.–5 p.m., Saturday 10 a.m.–7 p.m.

Popular with all ages, the science center's interactive exhibits bring science to life.

Heinz History Center

1212 Smallman St., Strip District

(412) 454-6000

www.pghhistory.org

Hours: Daily 10 a.m.–5 p.m.

The largest history museum in the state focuses primarily on the history of Pittsburgh.

Mattress Factory Art Museum

500 Sampsonia Way, North Side

(412) 231-3169

www.mattress.org

Hours: Tuesday–Saturday 10 a.m.–5 p.m., Sunday 1 p.m.–5 p.m.

One of the city's most unique attractions, this museum is dedicated to installation art.

National Aviary

700 Arch St., North Side

(412) 323-7235

www.aviary.org

Hours: Daily 10 a.m.–5 p.m.

The country's only independent indoor nonprofit aviary features more than 200 species of birds.

Phipps Conservatory and Botanical Gardens

1 Schenley Park, Oakland

(412) 622-6914

www.phipps.conservatory.org

Hours: Saturday–Thursday 9:30 a.m.–5 p.m., Friday 9:30 a.m.–10 p.m.

This steel and glass Victorian greenhouse has been open to visitors since 1893.

Pittsburgh Center for the Arts

6300 Fifth Ave., Shadyside

(412) 361-0873

www.pittsburgharts.org

Hours: Tuesday–Saturday 10 a.m.–5 p.m., Sunday 12 p.m.–5 p.m.

(Arts Center, continued)

This nonprofit community arts organization provides art education and exhibition.

Pittsburgh Filmmakers

477 Melwood Ave., Oakland

(412) 681-5449

www.pghfilmmakers.org

This nonprofit offers courses and exhibits works in theaters across Pittsburgh.

SPACE

812 Liberty Ave., Downtown

(412) 325-7723

www.spacepittsburgh.org

Hours: Tuesday–Thursday 11 a.m.–6 p.m., Friday–Saturday 11 a.m.–8 p.m.

This gallery displays a variety of works, including contemporary and installation pieces.

Wood Street Galleries

601 Wood St., Downtown

(412) 471-5605

www.woodstreetgalleries.org

Hours: Tuesday–Thursday 11 a.m.–6 p.m., Friday–Saturday 11 a.m.–8 p.m.

This gallery features multi-disciplinary artists from around the world.

Family-Friendly Entertainment:

Children's Museum of Pittsburgh

10 Children's Way, North Side

(412) 322-5058

www.pittsburghkids.org

Hours: Monday–Saturday 10 a.m.–5 p.m., Sunday 12 p.m.–5 p.m.

This museum has several hands-on exhibits and classes that let kids "play with real stuff."

Chuck E. Cheese's

3800 William Penn, Monroeville
(412) 856-5044

8100 McKnight Rd., North Hills
(412) 364-7762

www.chuckecheese.com

This place "where a kid can be a kid" has arcade games, rides, and attractions just for kids.

Dave & Buster's

180 E. Waterfront Dr., Homestead

(412) 462-1500

www.daveandbusters.com

D&B is a great place for adults and kids with games appropriate for most ages, as well as great food and a full-service bar for parents.

Duquesne Incline & Monongahela Incline

1220 Grandview Ave. or 5 Grandview Ave.
Mt. Washington

(Inclines, continued)

These historic cable cars travel up and down Mt. Washington and provide a spectacular view of Downtown and beyond.

Fun Fest Entertainment Center

2525 Freeport Rd., Harmarville

(412) 828-1100

www.funfestcenter.com

Glow bowling, laser tag, and arcade games—what more could a kid ask for?

Games N'at

2010 Josephine St., South Side

(412) 481-2002

www.gamesnat.com

Pittsburgh's largest video arcade also includes foosball, pinball, and skeeball, as well as a snack bar and live music.

Gateway Clipper Fleet

350 W. Station Square Dr. Station Square

(412) 355-7980

www.gatewayclipper.com

The Gateway Clipper is a great way to tour Pittsburgh's waterways—and learn stuff, too!

Idlewild & Soakzone

Route 30, Ligonier

(724) 238-6784

www.idlewild.com

Voted the second-best kid's park in the world, Idlewild's attractions include Story Book Forest.

Just Ducky Tours

125 W. Station Square Dr., Station Square

(412) 402-3825

www.justduckytours.com

This educational adventure tour takes riders throughout the city on both land and water.

Kennywood Park

4800 Kennywood Blvd. West Mifflin

(412) 461-0500

www.kennywood.com

This historic park's three wooden coasters and the steel Phantom's Revenge make it a mecca for roller coaster lovers.

Pittsburgh Zoo & PPG Aquarium

One Wild Place, Highland Park

(412) 665-3640

www.pittsburghzoo.com

One of only six major zoo-aquarium combinations in the country, the zoo is located near the northeastern edge of the city.

Sandcastle Waterpark

1000 Sandcastle Dr., Homestead

(412) 461-3694

www.sandcastlewaterpark.com

This waterpark boasts 14 water slides, several pools, and an adults-only section with a bar and "the world's largest hot tub."

Live Music Venues:

In addition to local bars that hold live music nights, these are the most popular venues to catch national acts and local bands.

31st Street Pub
3101 Penn Ave., Strip District
(412) 391-8334
www.31stpub.com

A.J. Palumbo Center
1302 Forbes Ave., Uptown
(412) 323-1919
www.duq.edu

Carnegie Music Hall of Homestead
510 E. 10th Ave., Munhall
(412) 432-3444
www.homesteadlibrary.org

Club Café
56 S. 12th St., South Side
(412) 431-4950
www.clubcafelive.com

Club Zoo
1630 Smallman St., Strip District
(412) 201-1100
www.clubzoo.net

Diesel Night Club
1601 E. Carson St., South Side
(412) 431-8800
www.liveatdiesel.com

Gravity Nightclub
1216 Pittsburgh St., Cheswick
(724) 715-7818

Hard Rock Café
230 W. Station Square Dr., Station Square
(412) 481-7625
www.hardrock.com

Mellon Arena
66 Mario Lemieux Pl., Downtown
(412) 642-1800
www.mellonarena.com

Mr. Small's Funhouse
400 Lincoln Ave., Millvale
(412) 821-4447
www.mrsmalls.com

Petersen Events Center
3719 Terrace St., Oakland
(412) 690-3901
www.peterseneventscenter.com

Post-Gazette Pavilion
Rt. 18 at Rt. 22, Burgettstown
(724) 947-7400
www.post-gazettepavilion.com

The Rex Theatre
1602 E. Carson St., South Side
(412) 381-6811
www.elkoconcerts.com

Shadow Lounge
5972 Baum Blvd., East Liberty
(412) 363-8277
www.shadowlounge.net

Movie Theaters

AMC Loews Waterfront 22
300 Waterfront Dr., Homestead
(412) 462-6384
www.amctheaters.com

Carmike Cinemas
1500 Washington Rd.
Mt. Lebanon
(412) 531-5551
2001 Mountain View Dr.
West Mifflin
(412) 655-8700
700 Fort Couch Rd.
Upper St. Clair
(412) 835-7074
629 Clairton Blvd., Pleasant Hills
(412) 655-3851
www.carmike.com

Cinemagic Theaters
1729 Murray Ave., Squirrel Hill
(412) 422-7729
5824 Forward Ave., Squirrel Hill
(412) 421-7900
www.cinemagicpgh.com

Dependable Drive-in
500 Moon-Clinton Rd.
Moon Twp.
(412) 264-7011
www.dependabledrivein.com

Destinta Theaters
1025 Washington Pike
Bridgeville
(412) 914-0999
1701 Lincoln Hwy.
North Versailles
(412) 824-9200
www.destinta.com

Showcase Cinemas
9700 McKnight Rd., North Hills
(724) 935-5885
Park Manor Dr., Robinson Twp.
(412) 787-5788
www.showcasecinemas.com

SouthSide Works Cinema
425 Cinema Dr., South Side
(412) 381-7335
www.southsideworks.com

Waterworks Cinema 10
930 Freeport Rd., Fox Chapel
(412) 784-1402

Performing Arts Venues:
Most local theaters and
performing groups are based in
the Cultural District downtown.

Benedum Center
719 Liberty Ave., Downtown
(412) 456-2600
www.pgharts.org

Byham Theater
101 Sixth St., Downtown
(412) 456-1350
www.pgharts.org

Cabaret at Theater Square
655 Penn Ave., Downtown
(412) 325-6769
www.clocabaret.com

City Theater Company
1300 Bingham St., South Side
(412) 431-2489
www.citytheatercompany.org

Dance Alloy Theater
5530 Penn Ave., East Liberty
(412) 363-4321
www.dancealloy.org

Heinz Hall
600 Penn Ave., Downtown
(412) 392-4900
www.pittsburghsymphony.org

Open Stage Theater
2835 Smallman St., Strip District
(412) 281-9700

Pittsburgh Ballet Theatre
2900 Liberty Ave., Downtown
(412) 281-0360
www.pbt.org

Pittsburgh Civic Light Opera
719 Liberty Ave., Downtown
(412) 281-3973
www.pittsburghclo.org

Pittsburgh Musical Theater
327 S. Main St., West End
(412) 539-0999
pittsburghmusicals.com

Pittsburgh Opera
2425 Liberty Ave., Downtown
(412) 281-0912
www.pittsburghopera.org

Pittsburgh Playhouse
222 Craft Ave., Oakland
(412) 621-4445
www.pointpark.edu

Pittsburgh Public Theater
621 Penn Ave., Downtown
(412) 434-7590
www.ppt.org

Other Places to Check Out:

Allegheny County Jail Museum
Cathedral of Learning
Fort Pitt Museum
Frick Art & Historical Center
Modern Formations
Pennsylvania Trolley Museum
Pittsburgh Glass Center
Pittsburgh Irish and Classical Theater
Three Rivers Arts Festival

Useful Resources for Arts & Entertainment

Pittsburgh City Paper
Pittsburgh Post-Gazette
Pittsburgh Tribune-Review
www.fandango.com
www.pgharts.com
www.ticketmaster.com

Did You Know?

Pittsburgh's Arts & Entertainment Firsts:

- The Ferris wheel was **invented by Pittsburgh-area bridge builder George Washington Gale Ferris** for the World's Columbian Exposition in Chicago in 1893. The first Ferris wheel stood over 250 feet tall and could carry 2,160 passengers in 36 cars.

- The first theater in the world **devoted exclusively to exhibiting motion pictures was the Nickelodeon**, which was opened on Smithfield Street in Pittsburgh in 1905.

- At 6 p.m. November 2, 1920, **KDKA Radio broadcast the U.S. presidential election returns** from a shack on top of a Westinghouse building in East Pittsburgh. KDKA claims to be the first commercial radio station in the country.

- WQED-Pittsburgh, **the first community-sponsored television station** in the country, was established April 1, 1954, after school children went door to door to collect $2 from families to help get the station on the air.

Movie Mecca?

Pittsburgh has played **host to more than 120 movie and television productions**. Some of the more popular ones are:

All the Right Moves (1983)
Angels in the Outfield (1951)
Boys on the Side (1995)
The Deer Hunter (1978)
Desperate Measures (1998)
Dogma (1999)
Flashdance (1983)
Groundhog Day (1993)
Gung Ho (1986)
Hoffa (1992)
Houseguest (1995)
Inspector Gadget (1999)
Kingpin (1996)
Lorenzo's Oil (1992)

Milk Money (1994)
The Mothman Prophecies (2002)
Night of the Living Dead (1968)
Only You (1994)
The Road (2009)
Robocop (1987)
Rock Star (2000)
The Silence of the Lambs (1991)
Slap Shot (1977)
Smart People (2006)
Striking Distance (1993)
Sudden Death (1995)
Wonder Boys (2000)
Zack & Miri Make a Porno (2008)

Locals Speak Out On...
Arts & Entertainment

"It's surprisingly good for a smaller city. There's a whole cultural district with several theaters that put on some really great shows. 'The Lion King,' 'Wicked,' and other great musicals have been here recently."

Q "We are extremely fortunate to have **such a vibrant cultural scene** for a mid-size city."

Q "The cultural atmosphere here is **the absolute best compared to any city of our size** and many larger! The variety and type of entertainment is unbelievable on a nightly basis."

Q "Pittsburgh is a very artistic and cultural city—which I think is surprising to many people. There are many plays, ballets, and symphonies showing all year long. **The museums are second-to-none in getting access to the hottest exhibits**. There is even the Carnegie Science Center, which is a great learning experience for children. The Phipps Conservatory is amazingly gorgeous and, in my opinion, is a hidden gem that more people need to go see! The summertime sees many ethnic festivals around the city."

Q "The North Side has a great number of cultural attractions. For modern art, **I recommend the Andy Warhol Museum and the Mattress Factory**."

Q "From live music to the ballet or the opera or even museums, **Pittsburgh really has it all**."

Q "It's very good for a city of this size. **The symphony, ballet, opera, and public theater are very well regarded**. There are lots of smaller theater and dance companies as well, and there is always something going on at the Byham, Benedum, Heinz Hall, or O'Reilly, as well as City Theater, Pittsburgh Irish and Classical Theater, and the Mattress Factory."

Q "Pittsburgh's cultural scene **can compete with any larger city in the country**. We have opera, ballet, symphony, Broadway shows, and plays."

Q "It's very good! There are **a lot of options and a lot of things happening** all the time."

Q "There is an endless supply of cultural activities in Pittsburgh, from the symphony to local bands, from art museums to play museums to history museums, and **from off-Broadway musicals to monster-truck rallies**. There is really something for everyone."

Q "Pittsburgh has a lot to offer that would surprise people! There is **much more in the music and theater scene**— symphony, opera, plays—but not much dance."

Q "Pittsburgh has a **better cultural scene than we have a right to expect**. Some of the bigger institutions, such as the symphony and opera, are holdovers from our bigger and richer days."

Q "It's decent. I don't get out to cultural events much, but **there is ballet, musical theater, great museums**, and the symphony."

The Urban Guru Take On...
Arts & Entertainment

The scope of Pittsburgh's cultural scene might surprise many people not familiar with the city, but locals have come to expect first-rate exhibits and entertainment. Pittsburgh regularly hosts a variety of national artists, and the city is almost always on tour itineraries for Broadway shows, popular musicians, and other national acts. The city has also been home to dozens of movie and television productions. The art culture in Pittsburgh is remarkable, offering access to both famous works by world-renowned artists at the Carnegie Museum of Art and modern and contemporary art by local, national, and international artists at galleries across the city.

Because the city is steeped in history, there is no shortage of cultural and educational activities for both children and adults to enjoy. The Heinz Regional History Center is a great place to start for a history of the Pittsburgh area, and a trip to the Carnegie Museum of Natural History is a must, especially for dinosaur lovers. Kids will love the interactive experience at the Carnegie Science Center and the Children's Museum. Not everything has to be about learning, though. Kennywood Amusement Park, Sandcastle Water Park, and several entertainment centers complete with arcades, bowling alleys, and other games make Pittsburgh fun for all ages.

The Urban Guru® Grade on

Arts & Entertainment: A

A high grade in Arts & Entertainment indicates that there are fun and interesting things to do, and that there is ample opportunity for cultural enrichment. Other factors include the presence of family friendly activities.

Sports & Recreation

The Lowdown On...
Sports & Recreation

Professional Teams:

Penguins

League: NHL

Web Site: *penguins.nhl.com*

Home Field: Mellon Arena in Uptown

Mascot: Iceburgh the penguin

Nicknames: Pens

Top Rivals: Philadelphia Flyers

Availability of Tickets: Penguins tickets have recently shot up in popularity—there are more than

(Penguins, continued)

2,500 people on the waiting list, which didn't exist until 2007—and getting tickets will probably be even harder once the new arena opens in 2010.

Best Moments: The Pens have made it to the playoffs 22 times, with back-to-back Stanley Cup wins in 1991 and 1992 and a trip to the finals in 2008.

Fun Fact: Sidney Crosby and other Penguins hand-delivered season tickets to a few lucky recipients' homes.

Pirates

League: MLB

Web Site: *pittsburgh.pirates.mlb.com*

Home Field: PNC Park on the North Shore

Mascot: Pirate Parrot, Captain Jolly Roger

Nicknames: Bucs, Buccos

Top Rivals: The Pirates don't have a true rival.

Availability of Tickets: Unless it's the home opener or a game with a popular opponent, you can usually get good seats moments before the first pitch. For every game Sunday–Thursday, $40 ($35 in advance) gets you an outfield seat and unlimited helpings of traditional stadium fare and soda.

Best Moments: There haven't been many good moments for the team lately, but PNC Park hosted the All-Star game in 2006. The Pirates have won five World Series titles, but the last was in 1979.

Fun Fact: During each home game, four runners dressed as large pierogies compete in the Great Pierogi Race.

Steelers

League: NFL

Web Site: *www.steelers.com*

Home Field: Heinz Field on the North Shore

Mascot: Steely McBeam

Nicknames: Black and Gold

Top Rivals: Cleveland Browns, Baltimore Ravens, and Cincinnati Bengals

Availability of Tickets: The Steelers have sold out every game since the 1972 season, and there is a 10-year waiting list for season tickets. The limited number of single-game tickets sold each season go fast.

Best Moments: The Steelers have won five Super Bowls, the last in 2005 when they beat the Seattle Seahawks 21–10.

Fun Fact: The Terrible Towel is synonymous with Steelers fans and Pittsburghers in general.

Pittsburgh Sports Blogs:

General: *doubtaboutit.com, mondesishouse.blogspot.com, psamp.blogspot.com, rizzosports.blogspot.com*

Penguins: *thepensblog.blogspot.com, igloodreams.blogspot.com*

Pirates: *bucsdugout.com, pittsburghpirates.buccoblog.com*

Steelers: *behindthesteelcurtain.com, steelersgab.com*

University of Pittsburgh: *pittblather.com*

Other Teams to Watch

Pitt Panthers Football
The University of Pittsburgh football team, which has produced such legends as Dan Marino, Mike Ditka, and Tony Dorsett, plays its home games at Heinz Field. Pitt has a long-standing rival with West Virginia, a fellow Big East Conference member. The Backyard Brawl, the game between these two teams, is one of the oldest college rivalries. Fun fact: After any Pitt victory, the upper section of the Cathedral of Learning on campus is illuminated gold, instead of the standard white.

Pitt Panthers Men's Basketball
The Pitt men's basketball team is a Big East power and the only team in conference history to reach the championship game seven times in eight seasons. Pitt is consistently ranked nationally and has made 20 NCAA Tournament appearances. Home games are played at the Petersen Events Center (aka "The Pete"), which regularly sells out every game.

Pitt Panthers Women's Basketball
The Pitt women's basketball team had a record-breaking season in 2007–08, finishing with its first postseason ranking in school history—16th. The team went to the NCAA Tournament the last two years and reached the Sweet Sixteen in 2008. Home games are also played at the Petersen Events Center.

Other College Teams
The teams of Duquesne University, Robert Morris University, and other local colleges are worth checking out for any sports fan.

High School Football
Most of the local football teams compete in the highly competitive Western Pennsylvania Interscholastic Athletic League (WPIAL), which consistently produces state champions in each division. Some traditional powerhouses include Central Catholic (where Dan Marino went to high school), Gateway, Jeannette (the alma mater of Terrelle Pryor, who was considered a top recruit in 2008 and went on to Ohio State), McKeesport, and Thomas Jefferson.

Ticket Resources

Before each season, the Steelers and Penguins release a limited number of single-game tickets to the general public via Ticketmaster. You can also check out the Steelers' Web site, where TicketExchange allows fans to resell game tickets, or you can try *CraigsList.org* or a ticket site like *StubHub.com*. Pirates tickets are easy to get through their Web site or at the PNC Park box office. University of Pittsburgh men's basketball tickets are tough to get, but there are always scalpers outside the Pete.

Gyms

AmeriFit Fitness Club

100 Roessler Rd., Green Tree
(412) 341-3033
afitspa.com
Cool Features: Aerobics classes, cardio room, handball, racquetball, spa, pilates/yoga
Hours: Monday–Thursday 5:30 a.m.–10 p.m., Friday 5:30 a.m.–9 p.m., Saturday–Sunday 8 a.m.–5 p.m.

Bally Total Fitness

119 Sixth St., Downtown
(412) 391-3300
www.ballyfitness.com
Cool Features: Juice bar, massage, personal trainers, pilates/yoga, pool, racquetball, sauna, track, tennis, whirlpool
Hours: Monday–Thursday 5:30 a.m.–10 p.m., Friday 5:30 a.m.–9 p.m., Saturday 8:30 a.m.–5 p.m., Sunday 8:30 a.m.–3 p.m.

Club One Fitness

6325 Penn Ave., Shadyside
(412) 362-4806
www.club1pittsburgh.com
Cool Features: Aerobics classes, café, pilates/yoga, personal trainers, pool
Hours: Monday–Thursday 5:45 a.m.–10 p.m., Friday 5:45 a.m.–9 p.m., Saturday–Sunday 8 a.m.–6 p.m.

East Carson Fitness

2504 E. Carson St., South Side
(412) 381-0797
Cool Features: New machines, free Wi-Fi, individual machine TVs, juice bar, personal trainers
Hours: Monday–Friday 5 a.m.–10 p.m., Saturday–Sunday 7 a.m.–7 p.m.

Fitness Factory

212 S. Highland Ave., Shadyside
(412) 362-6303
www.fitnessfactorypgh.com
Cool Features: Group classes, nutritional consulting, personal trainers, pilates/yoga

➡

(Fitness Factory, continued)
Hours: Monday–Thursday
7 a.m.–9 p.m.,
Friday 7 a.m.–8 p.m., Saturday–
Sunday 9 a.m.–4 p.m.

Gold's Downtown
100 Forbes Ave., Downtown
(412) 201-4653
*www.goldsgym.com/
pittsburghmarketsquarepa*
Cool Features: Group classes,
nutritionists, personal trainers,
pilates/yoga, sauna, tanning
Hours: Monday–Thursday
5 a.m.–11 p.m.,
Friday 5 a.m.–10 p.m.,
Saturday–Sunday 7 a.m.–8 p.m.

South Side Athletic Club
2026 E. Carson St., South Side
(412) 488-1120
Cool Features: This is a "no-
frills" gym for those who just
want to work out.
Hours: Monday–Friday
5 a.m.–9 p.m., Saturday–
Sunday 8 a.m.–4 p.m.

X Shadyside Health & Fitness
5608 Walnut St., Shadyside
(412) 363-9999
www.xshadyside.com
Cool Features: Group classes,
massage, monthly memberships,
pilates and yoga, tanning.
Hours: Daily 24 hours

Yoga Studios

Amazing Yoga
5823 Ellsworth Ave., Shadyside
(412) 661-1525
1506 E. Carson St., South Side
Opens Winter 2008.
11967 Perry Hwy., Wexford
(724) 935-2240
www.amazingyoga.net

Breathe Yoga Studio
1113 E. Carson St., South Side
(412) 481-YOGA
www.breathe-yogastudio.com

Schoolhouse Yoga
330 Grant St., Downtown
2401 Smallman St., Strip District
2010 Murray Ave., Squirrel Hill
5417 Walnut St., Shadyside
(412) 401-4444
www.schoolhouseyoga.com

Yoga on Centre
6016 Penn Cir. S., East Liberty
(412) 363-YOGA
www.yogaoncentre.com

Yoga on the Square
1112 S. Braddock Ave.,
Regent Square
(412) 287-4591
www.fitnessyoga.net

Pittsburgh Parks

Frick Park
At 600 acres, Frick is the city's largest park. There are plenty of trails perfect for hiking, biking, or walking your dog. You'll also find playgrounds, tennis courts, and a bowling green. The Frick Environmental Center offers workshops on topics like wreath making, nature photography, and birding.

Highland Park
Highland Park is home to the Pittsburgh Zoo and PPG Aquarium. There is also a three-quarter-mile walkway around a reservoir, a pool, a half-mile cycling track, trails, volleyball and tennis courts, and picnic shelters. For kids, there's a playground with a trolley ride, swings, slides, and a play phone system.

Mellon Park
This small park sits between Squirrel Hill and Shadyside. There are basketball courts, a tennis center enclosed in a climate-controlled "bubble," baseball fields, and a playground. You'll also find the Pittsburgh Center for the Arts here.

Point State Park
Located at the point where the Monongahela and Allegheny rivers form the Ohio River, Point State Park was once the site of the historic Fort Duquesne and Fort Pitt, which served pivotal roles in early conflicts over control of the region. Famous for its large fountain, Point State Park hosts many major events during the year, including Pittsburgh's July Fourth celebration.

Riverview Park
Riverview is tucked away just north of Downtown. While it doesn't get as much love as Frick or Schenley, there's still plenty to do—there is even an equestrian trail! You'll also find the Allegheny Observatory, a pool, baseball fields, picnic shelters, and a playground here.

Schenley Park
Schenley is one of the most popular parks in the city. Located in the heart of Oakland, it's a convenient destination for college students or anyone in the area checking out the nearby cultural attractions. In the park, you'll find a golf course, pool, skating rink, and lots of green space to enjoy.

Nearby Parks

Boyce Park

Boyce Park is about 15 miles east of Downtown in Plum/ Monroeville. Facilities include a wave pool, basketball and tennis courts, and plenty of open space to picnic or relax. In the winter, you can go skiing here.

North Park

North Park, located in Allison Park, is Allegheny County's largest park at 3,010 acres. It features a large lake, an ice skating rink, a pool, and a golf course. You can go hiking, fishing, or cross-country skiing or play baseball, horseshoes, or basketball.

South Park

The second-largest park in Allegheny County, located about 15 miles south of Downtown, South Park offers a golf course, an ice skating rink, tennis courts, a wave pool, and lots of trails to walk.

Outdoor Activities

Biking

You will find a lot of bikers in the city, but the nonlinear street patterns and hilly terrain can be intimidating, especially to newcomers. Don't be scared! There is a super helpful online Pittsburgh bike map (*map.bike-pgh.org*) that shows routes, trails, and even reported crashes or dangerous areas. You can also bike the Great Allegheny Passage, a series of seven interconnected trails stretching 150 miles from McKeesport, Pa. (neighboring Pittsburgh) to Cumberland, Md. These trails also run through the city along the shores of the Allegheny and Monongahela rivers.

Golfing

Golf courses in the Pittsburgh region range from reasonably priced public courses to prestigious country clubs—the most famous being the Oakmont Country Club, which has hosted numerous U.S. Opens. Other popular country clubs include Fox Chapel Golf Club, Longue Vue Country Club in Verona, Pittsburgh Field Club in Fox Chapel, St. Clair Country Club in Upper St. Clair, and Treesdale Golf and Country Club in Gibsonia. Popular public courses include those at Schenley and North parks and Meadowlink Golf Course in Monroeville. For more information, check out *www.post-gazette.com/sports/golf/courses*.

(Outdoor Activities, continued)

Hiking

The landscape in southwestern Pennsylvania is perfect for hiking—it is hilly and there are lots of forests. If you're looking to stay close to home, you can take short hikes on the trails in any of the city parks. For a more difficult hike, head about an hour and a half southeast to the Laurel Highlands, which has a 70-mile trail that runs through forests, game lands, and state parks. For a complete list of hiking trails in the area, check out *www.wallsarebad.com.*

Ice Skating

The Schenley Park Skating Rink is open all winter and hosts events like Skate with Santa and Mascot Skate, where you can skate with famous mascots from the region, such as Steely McBeam and the Eat-N-Park Smiley Cookie. The Schenley rink also offers special sessions for college students, adults, and families. The Rink at PPG Plaza downtown is a must see during the holidays, when the 60-foot-tall Christmas tree is lit up in the center of the rink, which is larger than the world-famous rink at Rockefeller Center in New York City. The rink is open from mid-November to early March, and skating lessons are available. There are also outdoor rinks in South and North parks, and Mellon Arena has special events where you can skate on a first-come, first-served basis.

Kayaking & Rowing

Pittsburgh is surrounded by three rivers, so kayaking and rowing opportunities are abundant. In the city, there is a flat-water kayak rental shop on the North Shore under the Roberto Clemente Bridge. Head toward The Point for a really different perspective of Downtown. For longer kayak trips, head to the Youghiogheny River or kayak from Saltsburg to Pittsburgh. If your interest lies more in rowing, you can join a rowing team—go to *www.threeriversrowing.org* for more information.

Recreational Sports

Sports are huge here, and if you're interested in playing a team sport, there are plenty of leagues you can get involved with. Pittsburgh Sports League offers adult intramural leagues in a variety of sports, including volleyball, softball, basketball, and more.

Skiing

You'll find a variety of ski resorts in the region, but two Pittsburgh favorites are Hidden Valley Resort and Seven Springs Mountain Resort, both located in the Laurel Highlands, about an hour east of the city. In addition to skiing, you can also go snowtubing, snowboarding, and snowmobiling here. Seven Springs has several different accommodation options from the large hotel to cabins and chalets. For skiing closer to home, head to Boyce Park, which offers the only downhill skiing in Allegheny County.

Swimming

There are 18 Citiparks outdoor pools, so there's likely one convenient to where you live. The city pools are open to everyone, but residents of the City of Pittsburgh receive a discount on pool tag fees. Another great place to cool off is Sandcastle Waterpark, which features 14 waterslides, pools for adults and kids, a wave pool, and the Lazy River. If you want to swim during the fall, winter, or spring, head to the Oliver Bath House on the South Side, which is the city's only indoor pool.

Tennis

There are tennis courts scattered throughout the city, as well as several leagues you can join. Check out the Citiparks Tennis Program, which offers lessons, programs, and tournaments. For indoor play, head to the "bubble" in Mellon Park.

Did You Know?

 A Brookings Institution survey **ranked Pittsburgh as the ninth most walkable city** according to the number of "walkable urban places" relative to the population.

Favorite Golf Courses/ Country Clubs:

Oakmont Country Club

Fox Chapel Field Club

St. Clair Country Club

Favorite Gyms:

Club One Fitness

East Carson Fitness

Fitness Factory

Favorite Outdoor Activity:

Biking

Kayaking

Favorite Parks:

Schenley Park

Frick Park

Favorite Places to Take a Walk:

Any of the city parks, especially Frick or Schenley

North Shore Riverwalk

Trails in the South Side or on Washington's Landing

Favorite Places to Watch the Game:

Bars on the North Shore, especially McFadden's and Jerome Bettis' Grille 36

Buffalo Blues, Shadyside

Heinz Field

PNC Park

Favorite Place for Winter Sports:

Seven Springs

Favorite Place to Tailgate:

Heinz Field parking lot

Favorite Tennis Courts:

Mellon Park

Schenley Park

Favorite Yoga Studio:

Amazing Yoga

Did You Know?

Fun Facts about Pittsburgh Sports:

- All three professional **sports teams in Pittsburgh wear black and gold**. The Penguins originally wore blue and white but switched over to their current colors in 1980.

- PNC Park is **consistently listed among the best ballparks in the country**—in 2006, ESPN rated it as the best in the nation.

- **The Pittsburgh Steelers have never retired any numbers**, but certain ones are never handed out to new players: 12 (Terry Bradshaw), 31 (Donnie Shell), 32 (Franco Harris), 47 (Mel Blount), 52 (Mike Webster), 58 (Jack Lambert), 59 (Jack Ham), 70 (Ernie Stautner), and 75 (Joe Greene).

- The Penguins' **logo features a skating penguin on top of a gold triangle, which represents the Golden Triangle**—another name for Downtown Pittsburgh.

Famous Sports Figures from Pittsburgh:

Kurt Angle, Marc Bulger, Swin Cash, Mark Cuban, Mike Ditka, Terry Francona, Jim Furyk, Ken Griffey Jr. and Sr., Jim Kelly, Ryan Malone, Dan Marino, Bill Mazeroski, Suzie McConnell-Serio, Rocco Mediate, Joe Montana, Joe Namath, Arnold Palmer, Jason Taylor, Johnny Unitas, and Honus Wagner.

Pittsburgh Sports Firsts:

- **The first World Series game was between the Pirates and Boston** in 1903. The Pirates lost in nine games.

- The **first World Series night game was also played in Pittsburgh** between the Pirates and the Baltimore Orioles October 13, 1971. The Pirates won the series.

- Forbes Field, **the first baseball stadium**, was built in the city's Oakland neighborhood in 1909. It was demolished in 1971.

- Mellon Arena, built in 1961, was the world's **first domed building with a retractable roof**.

Locals Speak Out On...
Sports & Recreation

"Pittsburghers are crazy about sports. The Steelers get most of the attention, but the Pens have a huge following as well. The Pirates suck every year, but the stadium is beautiful and worth a trip."

"Football, football, and more football! The Steelers are a big deal, and **hockey is growing even more popular**. Baseball is fun, mostly because of the ballpark. College sports are not as popular as major league teams here."

"If you don't like the Pens or the Steelers, watch your back! Either join in on the fun or quietly keep to yourself because **Pittsburgh breeds some of the most hardcore and dedicated fans around**."

"The Pittsburgh sports scene is the best! **Definitely go to a Steelers game for the all-around energy** of the people—plus the tailgating is great!"

"If you're not a Steelers fan, **don't expect much love at the sports bars**."

"The pride and joy of Pittsburgh right now is the Penguins. **It is rare to go out and not see a Crosby or Malkin jersey**. Everyone will root for the Steelers 'til the end though. The Pirates are a bit of a joke."

"Pittsburgh's sports scene is probably the best of any city! Pittsburghers are very loyal to their sports teams, especially the Steelers and Penguins. **I've never seen so many people rally behind a common interest!**"

Q "Baseball fans are **almost nonexistent**."

Q "The Steelers are usually good. The Pens are good now. **The Pirates have stunk for ages**."

Q "I didn't grow up in this area, so I'm not a Steelers fan at all, and I don't think I ever will be because **the fans are so die hard**—I don't think I could just 'become' a fan."

Q "**Baseball games are really fun to go to** because of the great stadium and cheap tickets, but the team sucks."

Q "It is intensely Steelers—and football in general. **The town shuts down during game time on Sundays**. Pittsburghers support the Penguins and Pirates as well but only if they are doing well. Steelers receive full support even if they suck."

Q "**The Steelers' season is annoying** because everyone is so protective of their team and pisses on anyone who doesn't think highly of them."

Q "Pittsburgh is a **drinking town with a football problem**."

Q "Welcome to Steelers Nation. Do we have a baseball team or a just great baseball stadium for concerts and fireworks shows? The Pens are awesome. Sidney Crosby is really developing as a great player. **There's always a fun atmosphere at the Pens games**—it's always a sellout, and the fans are great to be around. I can't wait for the new arena."

Q "Love the Steelers or die—I'm pretty sure that's their motto. **They literally bleed black and gold in this city**. If you don't believe me, cut a Pittsburgher's arm and see the mess that comes out."

Q "Sure, the Steelers have a die-hard following, but **my favorite is watching the Pens**!"

Q "**Pittsburgh will never be confused with a basketball city, but Pitt is emerging as a national power**. Petersen Events Center could be louder, but there are no bad seats, and the quality of the opponents is usually good."

Q "We love sports, but **if you don't like them, don't worry, no one will hurt you**."

Q "There are **lots of local groups that organize amateur sports leagues**, and there are plenty of public facilities across the city."

Q "**You'd better have your Steelers jersey** on the day of the game!"

Q "Pittsburgh is hands down the **best sports town in the country**."

Q "People in Pittsburgh love their sports, and they're very passionate about them. The main team here is, of course, the Steelers. Once the season starts, that's all you'll hear people talking about, and you'll see people wearing black and gold everywhere. We also have a really good hockey team and **a beautiful baseball park, even if the team isn't the best**."

Q "**You bleed black and gold after a few years** of living in Pittsburgh."

Q "Frick Park is nice and wooded, and when you're running or mountain biking on the trails, **you don't feel like you're in the city**."

The Urban Guru Take On...
Sports & Recreation

Pittsburgh is a very sports-centric city, and fans here are very loyal, especially Steelers supporters, who can be found waving their Terrible Towels at away games across the country. In fact, *ESPN.com* named Steelers fans the best in the league, and it's not just men who rally behind the Steelers. According to a *USA Today* survey, Pittsburgh has the highest percentage of female football fans in the country. Sidney Crosby and the Penguins are also gaining a lot of fan support, and tickets are getting to be just as hard to snag as Steelers tickets. The Pirates don't get as much love, mostly because they aren't very good. But PNC Park is amazing—the views of Downtown are awesome, there aren't any bad seats in the house, and tickets are affordable, so it's definitely worth it to go to a game. If you like basketball, the University of Pittsburgh usually has one of the top men's teams in the nation.

Pittsburgh also has lots of great outdoor spaces in and around the city where you can do everything from walk your dog to play tennis, and the parks aren't just fun in the warm months. Several have ice skating rinks, and Boyce Park even has downhill skiing. Whether you prefer to watch or participate, Pittsburgh is the perfect city for people who like sports.

The Urban Guru® Grade on
Sports and
Recreation: A+

A high grade in Sports and Recreation indicates that locals are supportive of their teams, the sports teams are respected, games are well-attended, and there are plenty of places to participate in sports, such as parks and gyms.

Shopping

The Lowdown On...
Shopping

Popular Malls:

Century III Mall

3075 Clairton Rd., West Mifflin

www.century-3-mall.com

Hours: Monday–Saturday
10 a.m.–9:30 p.m.,
Sunday 11 a.m.–6 p.m.

Distance from Downtown:
8 miles south

Main Stores: Aeropostale,
American Eagle, JCPenney,
Macy's, NY & Co., Old Navy,
Sears, Wet Seal

(Century III, continued)

Food: Typical mall fare like
Auntie Anne's Pretzels, Orange
Julius, Subway

Galleria at Pittsburgh Mills

590 Pittsburgh Mills Circle
Tarentum

www.pittsburghmills.com

Hours: Monday–Thursday
10 a.m.–9 p.m., Friday–
Saturday 10 a.m.–9:30 p.m.,
Sunday 11 a.m.–6 p.m.

Distance from Downtown:
20 miles north

➜

(Pittsburgh Mills, continued)

Main Stores: Aeropostale, American Eagle, Borders, Forever 21, H&M, JCPenney, Macy's, Sears Grand, Wet Seal

Food: Houlihan's, Johnny Rockets, Marble Slab Creamery, Orange Julius, Panera Bread

Cool Features: There's a carousel and an IMAX theater.

The Mall at Robinson

100 Robinson Centre Dr. Robinson

www.shoprobinsonmall.com

Hours: Monday–Saturday 10 a.m.–9:30 p.m., Sunday 11 a.m.–6 p.m.

Distance from Downtown: 15 miles south

Main Stores: Abercrombie & Fitch, Aeropostale, American Eagle, Banana Republic, Buckle, Eddie Bauer, Express, Gap, H&M, Hollister, JCPenney, Macy's, NY & Co., Sears, Wet Seal

Food: Charley's Grilled Subs, Chick-fil-A, Little Tokyo, Max Orient, Orange Julius, Villa Pizza

Monroeville Mall

Business Route 22, Monroeville

www.monroevillemall.com

Hours: Monday–Saturday 10 a.m.–9:30 p.m., Sunday 12 p.m.–6 p.m.

Distance from Downtown: 15 miles east

Main Stores: Abercrombie & Fitch, American Eagle, Arden B,

(Monroeville Mall, continued)

Buckle, Forever 21, Gap, Guess, JCPenney, Macy's, Nine West, NY & Co., White House/Black Market, Wet Seal

Food: Sawa Japanese Steak House, Carino's Italian Grill, Houlihan's, Monterey Bay Fish Grotto

Ross Park Mall

1000 Ross Park Mall Dr., Ross

www.ross-park-mall.com

Hours: Monday–Saturday 10 a.m.–9:30 p.m., Sunday 11 a.m.–6 p.m.

Distance from Downtown: 10 miles northeast

Main Stores: Abercrombie & Fitch, Banana Republic, Coach, Forever 21, Gap, H&M, Hollister, J. Crew, JCPenney, L.L. Bean, Louis Vuitton, Lucky Brand, Macy's, Nine West, Nordstrom, Old Navy, Pottery Barn, Sephora, Tiffany & Co., White House Black Market, Williams-Sonoma

Food: Cheesecake Factory, Chick-fil-A, Kelly's Cajun Grill, Manchu Wok, Sakkio Japan, Villa Pizza

South Hills Village

Washington Road, Bethel Park

www.south-hills-village.com

Hours: Monday–Saturday 10 a.m.–9:30 p.m., Sunday 11 a.m.–6 p.m.

Distance from Downtown: 7 miles south

Main Stores: Abercrombie & Fitch, Aeropostale, American

(South Hills Village, continued)

Eagle, Banana Republic, Buckle, Coach, Gap, Hollister, J. Crew, The Limited, Lucky Brand, Macy's, NY & Co., Sears, Sephora, Wet Seal, White House/Black Market

Food: Au Bon Pain, Cajun Café, Eat 'n' Park, Panda Express, Rita's Italian Ice, Sakkio Japan, Subway, Taco Bell, Villa Fresh

Popular Shopping Districts:

Shadyside

Ellsworth Avenue, South Aiken Avenue, and Walnut Street

www.shadysideshops.com

Distance from Downtown: 5 miles east

Overview: Shadyside is the place for upscale boutiques. Walnut Street has many higher-end chain stores, and Ellsworth features local stores and galleries.

Main Stores: American Apparel, Ann Taylor, Apple, Banana Republic, Benetton, Coach, J. Crew, Williams-Sonoma

Food: There are lots of cafés, coffee shops, and restaurants, including the Elbow Room, Harris Grill, and Walnut Grill.

Shops at Station Square

Intersection of Smithfield Street Bridge and East Carson Street.

www.stationsquare.com

Hours: Monday–Saturday 10 a.m.–9 p.m., Sunday 12 p.m.–5 p.m.

(Station Square, continued)

Distance from Downtown: 1 mile south, across Mon River

Overview: A tourist hotspot, Station Square is home to the Gateway Clipper and both inclines in addition to its many stores, restaurants, and bars.

Main Stores: Accentricity Fashion Jewelry, Morini's, Heinz Healey's, Jezebel's, New York, NY, St. Brendan's Crossing, Soxx Shop

Food: More than 20 eateries, including Bar Louie, Buckhead Saloon, Kiku Japanese Restaurant, The Melting Pot, Pittsburgh Rare, and Sesame Inn.

SouthSide Works

Between 26th and Hot Metal streets on the South Side

www.southsideworks.com

Distance from Downtown: 3 miles southeast

Overview: One of the newer shopping and entertainment complexes is also home to the global headquarters of American Eagle Outfitters and an 11-screen movie multiplex.

Main Stores: American Eagle Outfitters, Ann Taylor Loft, BCBG Max Azria, Benetton, Forever 21, H&M, Nine West, Puma, REI, Steve Madden, Urban Outfitters, White House/Black Market, Z Gallerie

Food: Cheesecake Factory, Claddagh Irish Pub, Dolce, McCormick & Schmick's Seafood Restaurant, Pita Pit, Qdoba Mexican Grill, Rosa NY Style Pizza, Tusca Global Tapas

The Waterfront

E. Waterfront Dr., Homestead

Hours: Monday–Saturday
10 a.m.–9:30 p.m.,
Sunday 11 a.m.–6 p.m.

Distance from Downtown:
8 miles east

Overview: This open-air shopping and entertainment complex was built on land once occupied by a U.S. Steel plant.

Main Stores: Barnes & Noble, Best Buy, DSW, Filene's Basement, Loews Cineplex, Macy's, Marshall's, Michaels, Old Navy, Target, TJ Maxx

Food: Bravo! Cucina Italiana, Dave & Busters, Mitchell's Fish Market, P.F. Chang's China Bistro, Rock Bottom Brewery, Yokoso Japanese Steak House

Boutiques:

Chick Downtown

717 Liberty Ave., Downtown
(866) 45-CHICK

www.chickdowntown.com

Cool Features: Clothes from this boutique are regularly featured in national fashion magazines like Elle, InStyle, and Lucky.

e.b. Pepper

5411 Walnut St., Shadyside
(412) 683.3815

www.ebpepper.net

Cool Features: Since 1987, this clothing boutique has featured lines from Europe.

Equita

3609 Butler St., Lawrenceville
(412) 353-0109

www.shopequita.com

Cool Features: Equita sells only products and food items that are fair-trade, "green," and sweatshop-free.

Hip'tique

5817 Ellsworth Ave., Shadyside
(412) 361-5817

Cool Features: This shop carries a nice selection of women's clothing, handbags, and jewelry.

Jupe Boutique

2306 E. Carson St., South Side
(412) 432-7933

www.jupeboutique.com

Cool Features: Named for the French word for skirt, Jupe offers styles from emerging designers.

Palm Place

732 Filbert St., Shadyside
(412) 683-5530

Cool Features: Palm Place is the only Lilly Pulitzer signature store in the tri-state area.

Pittsburgh Jeans Company

2222 E. Carson St., South Side
(412) 381-JEAN

pittsburghjeanscompany.com

Cool Features: Come here to get custom-fit jeans, or just send your measurements, and they'll mail your altered jeans.

Sugar Boutique

3703 Butler St., Lawrenceville
(412) 681-5100

5890 Ellsworth Ave., Shadyside
(412) 404-8850

www.sugarboutique.com

Cool Features: Sugar features clothing from local designers as well as new designers from across the country.

Computers:

Apple

5508 Walnut St., Shadyside
(412) 683-1186
apple.com/retail/shadyside

Gifts/Specialty:

The Bead Mine

1703 E. Carson St., South Side
(412) 381-8822

www.thebeadmine.net

Cool Features: Tons of unique beads and offers jewelry-making classes and workshops.

Culture Shop

1602 E. Carson St., South Side
(412) 481-8284

Cool Features: Gift ideas here include handmade clothes, journals, jewelry, and exotic decorations with Far Eastern flair.

S.W. Randall Toys and Gifts

630 Smithfield St., Downtown
(412) 562-9252

806 Ivy St., Shadyside
(412) 687-2666

5856 Forbes Ave., Squirrel Hill
(412) 422-7009

www.swrandalltoys.com

Cool Features: Pittsburgh's largest toy store has more than 20,000 items in stock.

Home Décor:

Artistry

2613 Smallman St., Strip District
(412) 765-2522

Cool Features: This unique shop sells home and garden accents in many styles.

Hot Haute Hot

2124 Penn Ave., Strip District
(412) 338-2323

www.hothautehot.com

Cool Features: This high-end store has one-of-a-kind pieces from hand-blown light fixtures to vintage desks.

IKEA

2001 Park Manor Blvd. Robinson
(412) 747-0747

www.ikea.com

Cool Features: The Pittsburgh IKEA offers child-care services, a restaurant, and a food market.

Perlora

2220 E. Carson St., South Side

(412) 431-2220

perlora.com

Cool Features: Voted best furniture store by the readers of Pittsburgh's *City Paper*.

Z Gallerie

510 S. 27th St., South Side

(412) 432-5770

www.zgallerie.com

Cool Features: Z Gallerie sells unique artwork, bedding, furniture, and accessories.

Jewelry:

Frost & Co.

717 Liberty Ave., Downtown

(412) 471-2234

www.frostdiamonds.com

Gems of the World

2023 E. Carson St., South Side

(412) 432-0300

Henne Jewelers

5501 Walnut St., Shadyside

(412) 682-0226

www.hennejewelers.com

Orr's Jewelers

5857 Forbes Ave., Squirrel Hill

(412) 421-6777

www.orrsrocks.com

Trinity Jewelers

647 Mount Nebo Rd.
North Hills

(412) 367-7131

www.trinityjewelers.com

Men's Suits:

Brooks Brothers

600 Smithfield St., Downtown

(412) 471-2300

www.brooksbrothers.com

Cool Features: Locations at the airport, Pittsburgh Mills Mall, and the new Tanger Outlets.

Larrimor's

501 Grant St., Downtown

(412) 471-5727

Cool Features: Larrimor's is the place to go for a nice suit. There are also in-house tailors.

Saks Fifth Avenue

513 Smithfield St., Downtown

(412) 263-4800

www.saksfifthavenue.com

Cool Features: This Saks is small compared to other locations, but the selection is nice.

Music:

Dave's Music Mine

1210 E. Carson St., South Side

(412) 488-8800

www.davesmusicmine.com

➜

(Dave's Music, continued)

Cool Features: Dave's has new and used music and movies and can special-order anything.

Eides Entertainment

1121 Penn Ave., Downtown
(412) 261-0900

www.eides.com

Cool Features: This three-level store sells CDs, records, comic books, movies, and T-shirts.

Jerry's Records

2136 Murray Ave., Squirrel Hill
(412) 421-4533

www.jerrysrecords.com

Cool Features: Jerry's has rows and rows of records from all decades and genres.

Paul's Compact Discs

4526 Liberty Ave., Bloomfield
(412) 621-3256

members.aol.com/paulsstore

Cool Features: Paul's sells both new and used CDs and tickets to local concerts.

Record Village

5519 Walnut St., Shadyside
(412) 682-1984

Cool Features: Choices include everything from Top 40 to Latin and African music.

Shoes:

Footloose

736 Bellefonte St., Shadyside
(412) 687-3663

Galleria of Mt. Lebanon
(412) 531-9663

footlooseshoesalon.com

Cool Features: Footloose carries some of the top shoe designers like Stuart Weitzman.

Littles Super Shoe Store

5850 Forbes Ave., Squirrel Hill
(800) 646-SHOE

www.littlesshoes.com

Cool Features: Littles specializes in hard-to-find sizes and widths for men, women, and children.

Pavement

3629 Butler St., Lawrenceville
(412) 621-6400

www.pavementshoes.com

Cool Features: This cute boutique has lots of original, unique shoes and brands that you can't find anywhere else in Pittsburgh.

Ten Toes

5502 Walnut St., Shadyside
(412) 683-2082

Cool Features: There's a big selection of style and brands, but they're also affordable so you can get more than one pair.

Vintage/Consignment:

Ambiance

1039 S. Braddock Ave.
Regent Square

(412) 243-5523

www.ambianceboutique.org

Cool Features: Proceeds help homeless women find housing through the non-profit organization Bethlehem Haven.

Avalon Exchange

5858 Forbes Ave., Squirrel Hill

(412) 421-2911

www.avalonexchange.com

Cool Features: Bring in items to trade in or exchange for cash.

Eons Fashion Antique

5850 Ellsworth Ave., Shadyside

(412) 361-3368

Cool Features: You can find stuff here for any occasion, and some items are still in their original packaging with tags.

Hey Betty!

5892 Ellsworth Ave., Shadyside

(412) 363-0999

Cool Features: No matter what you're looking for—1950s dresses, retro tees, ball gowns, jeans, coats, jewelry—you can find it here.

Did You Know?

Ross Park Mall recently transformed itself into a **swanky shopping destination** with the addition of several high-end stores, including:

BCBG Max Azria	Lucky Brand
Buckle	Martin + Osa
Burberry	Michael Kors
Clarks	Nordstrom
Janie & Jack	Tiffany & Co.
Juicy Couture	True Religion Jeans
Kate Spade	White House/
L.L. Bean	Black Market
Louis Vuitton	

Locals' Favorite Places to Shop:
Ross Park Mall
South Side/SouthSide Works
Shadyside
The Waterfront

Best Casual Clothes:
Urban Outfitters in the
SouthSide Works

Best Home Décor or Furniture:
Hot Haute Hot

Best Jeans:
Pittsburgh Jeans Co.

Best Jewelry:
Henne Jewelers
Orr's Jewelers
Tiffany's

Best Men's Suits:
Larrimor's

Best Shoes:
Ten Toes

Best Vintage Clothes:
Avalon Exchange

Best Work Clothes:
United Colors of Benetton
in Shadyside

Outlet Malls

Prime Outlets Grove City
There are more than 120 brand-name outlet stores in this mall, about 50 miles north of Pittsburgh on Interstate 79. You'll find Ann Taylor, Banana Republic, Coach, Gap, J. Crew, Nautica, Nike, Old Navy, Polo Ralph Lauren, Reebok, and Tommy Hilfiger, just to name a few. Recent additions include aerie by American Eagle and Juicy Couture. For a complete store listing, visit *www.primeoutlets.com.*

Tanger Outlets, Washington, Pa.
The area's newest outlet mall opened in Summer 2008. Located about 30 minutes south of Pittsburgh, these outlets feature more than 75 stores that include Calvin Klein, Converse, Nine West, and Puma.

Best-Kept Shopping Secrets

All-Clad Biannual Sale

All-Clad, the high-quality cookware used by chefs around the world, is based in Canonsburg, about 30 minutes from Pittsburgh. The company holds a biannual factory sale where you can get beautiful pots and pans for between 40 and 70 percent off. Inspect each one for serious damage before buying, but most only have minor scratches.

Construction Junction

Construction Junction is a local organization that sells recycled and surplus building materials, and it's the place to go if you are renovating or restoring a home. The constantly changing stock generally includes appliances, doors, furniture, hardware, tile and flooring, windows, and much more. Stop by their store on North Lexington Street in Point Breeze or check out what they have online at *www.constructionjunction.org.*

Lenox Outlet

For a great deal on Lenox china and glassware, visit the outlet center in Mount Pleasant. It's a bit of a hike from Pittsburgh—about 40 miles southeast—but you can save a bundle on discontinued and overstocked items.

Sears Outlets

If you're in the market for appliances, head to one of the Sears Outlets, where you can get appliances with scratches and dents—most are very small—for up to half off. There's an outlet in Lawrenceville and one in Bridgeville, about 10 miles south of the city.

Did You Know?

Pennsylvania's state sales tax is 6 percent, and Allegheny County's is 7 percent. However, most **clothing items are exempt from sales tax**.

If you're looking for jewelry, head downtown to the Clark Building on Liberty Avenue—**it houses more than 20 jewelers**.

Locals Speak Out On...
Shopping

"In terms of the shopping in the city, it's pretty good. There are several malls nearby, and there are lots of city shopping districts that have a mix of boutiques and mainstream stores."

Q "Shopping districts are popping up everywhere lately, but I really appreciate Ross Park Mall in the North Hills. **It is constantly getting new, great high-end stores** like Louis Vuitton, Burberry, True Religion, BCBG, and Nordstrom, with more to come."

Q "Monroeville Mall is a great indoor mall. It has been updated over the years to include many modern stores. Also, the Mall at Robinson is very nice, and **the area of Robinson in general is growing very fast** with lots of shopping and dining."

Q "When I go to a mall, I usually only go to Urban Outfitters, Forever 21, and H&M, so lucky for me, SouthSide Works has all three stores within a one-block radius of one another, so it's perfect. There is also a movie theater and a Cheesecake Factory, so **I can pretty much spend the whole day there without getting bored**."

Q "Walnut Street in Shadyside is my favorite shopping area. I love it because they have Banana Republic and Sephora, which are two of my favorite stores! **There are also a lot of really cute, small shops**. It's a really good shopping atmosphere."

Q "Skip the malls—they are all the same. **Shadyside has the most unique shopping** in the area."

Q "**The Waterfront has most of what you'll need**. Downtown has a good Macy's, and there is an outlet mall that's not far."

Q "I go to either Ross Park Mall or The Waterfront. **Ross Park has a lot of stores I would be willing to shop from**, and The Waterfront has shops and big-time stores like Costco and Marshall's."

Q "The malls in **Monroeville and Robinson are my favorites**."

Q "There is a **really good outlet in Grove City, which is about an hour to an hour-and-a-half drive** from the city."

Q "My favorite shopping district in Pittsburgh is the South Side. The SouthSide Works offers many popular stores and chains, as well as some high-end stores, and the **stores on Carson Street are perfect for finding funky or unique items**."

Q "Construction Junction is a **great place to find recycled renovation treasures** and to donate your old construction materials."

Q "SouthSide Works is the perfect 'one stop' for an **awesome selection in clothes, home décor, and books**."

Q "Ross Park Mall is the best because it's the easiest to get to, and **it has the most variety of stores in one place**."

Q "Avalon Exchange is amazing. **You can sell your old clothes for cash or store credit**, and the selection there is great for a cheap price. They have vintage items and stuff that you would find at Urban Outfitters, H&M, and stores along those lines."

Q "Some of the little boutiques on the South Side have **hidden treasures if you're willing to look around**."

Q "Robinson offers any store you can imagine, but **Shadyside and Ross Park Mall offer higher-end stores that are not available in Robinson**. The SouthSide Works also offers a nice outdoor shopping area."

Q "I love the boutiques in Shadyside. Also, if you don't mind a bit of a drive, **the outlets in Grove City are worth a look**. Going to school so close to the outlets began my unfortunate Coach addiction."

Q "Filene's Basement in The Waterfront has **high-quality clothes at basement prices**."

Q "**Shadyside has nice upscale shopping**. Robinson has a nice mall. The SouthSide Works is also nice."

Q "If you are looking for a mall scene, Robinson is good, and **the SouthSide Works is really picking up**. The Waterfront is also a good location for an outdoor mall."

The Urban Guru Take On...
Shopping

No one would ever confuse Pittsburgh with New York City when it comes to shopping, but for a smaller city, the options are really great here. There's a good mix of high-end boutiques, malls, and shopping centers sprinkled throughout the city and nearby suburbs. You'll find all the popular chain stores—including a newly opened Nordstrom in Ross Park Mall and an IKEA in the South Hills—but there are also tons of independently owned shops that sell everything: hard-to-find and one-of-a-kind clothing items, vintage pieces, shoes, handmade jewelry, and home décor.

And the shopping options in Pittsburgh just keep getting better. The SouthSide Works opened a couple of years ago to quickly become one of the city's most popular shopping destinations, and Ross Park Mall in the North Hills is constantly attracting high-end designer stores, many of which can't be found anywhere else in Pittsburgh, such as Burberry, Juicy Couture, Michael Kors, and Tiffany & Co. If you're looking for a deal, head to the Grove City outlets, which are only about an hour and half from Pittsburgh and offer plenty of stores to choose from.

The Urban Guru® Grade on
Shopping: B+

A high grade in Shopping indicates there are plenty of shopping options such malls, independently owned stores, and shopping areas, and that new stores are continually coming to the area.

Dating & Social Life

The Lowdown On...
Dating & Social Life

Percentage of Men:
48%

Percentage of Women:
52%

**Marital Status
(Age 15 and up):**
Single: 40%
Married: 38%
Divorced: 9%

Social Scene

Social life in Pittsburgh revolves mostly around the local nightlife, but there are plenty of options for anyone who isn't into the bar or club scene. Sporting and cultural events are great places to meet new people, whether you're looking for a date or just a new friend. Pittsburghers are generally friendly and outgoing, so the only rule is to be yourself.

Dress Code

In general, Pittsburgh is a laid-back town, and the dress code reflects that. It's perfectly acceptable at most restaurants, bars, and clubs to walk in wearing a T-shirt and jeans. Of course, you'll always see scantily clad women dressed to the nines for a night on the town, and there are some clubs with strict dress codes. Most Pittsburghers, though, would prefer to ditch the fancy pretense for a more casual approach, but that doesn't mean they can't be fashionable at the same time.

Best Places to Take a Date

Andy Warhol Museum

Benedum Center

Carnegie Museums of Art and History

Carnegie Science Center/UPMC Sportsworks

Comedy clubs like the Improv and Funny Bone

Dueling piano bars like Sing Sing and Charlie Murdoch's

Duquesne or Monongahela incline

The Mattress Factory

The National Aviary

Phipps Conservatory

Did You Know?

Forbes.com ranked Pittsburgh **ninth for Best Cities for Couples** based on marriage and divorce rates for 20- to 34-year-olds, affordability of starter homes, income disparity, and availability of family counseling.

Locals Speak Out On...
Dating & Social Life

"It's not the greatest. The bad thing is that Pittsburgh is a really small town. Oftentimes, it's hard not to run into an ex, a one-night stand, or someone you don't really want to run into!"

"It's not bad. I met my fiancé here! **I'd say bars, intramural events, or work** are the best places to meet people here."

"The singles scene is good. **It's not difficult to meet people at a bar**, and there are a lot of bars to go to. If one is lame, the bar next door is probably good."

"Harris Grill and Shady Grove are places where you'll likely run into graduate students and young professionals in the area. **Avoid Station Square, unless you want an undergraduate student scene**."

"Singles are hard to find unless you know where to look. Try the upscale bars in the South Side. Otherwise, you may **find yourself in a saloon with a bunch of dudes** for the rest of the night."

"The singles scene could use some help; **actually, it needs to be resuscitated**. When I was living in the Boston and Providence areas, the singles scenes were much better. Hopefully the city can revitalize the area with the casino and the new Penguins arena to get more younger people back in Pittsburgh."

"It's a horrible place to meet singles **if you're not white**."

Q "**If you don't like going to bars, you're probably going to have a difficult time** meeting other singles in Pittsburgh."

Q "I would say just go out a lot—not necessarily "out" to a bar or something, but **get involved in different things in the community** so you have the opportunity to meet a lot of new people."

Q "Pittsburgh is a small town, and **you see the same people all the time, for better or worse**."

Q "**Pittsburgh is swarming with singles ready to mingle**. It's unreal how many people are out at night waiting to make a 'friend.' But it's not just the bar scene—my good friend met his girlfriend while playing tennis at Schenley Park one day."

Q "It seems like almost every guy I've met here is single, which is obviously a great thing for the single ladies. But **nearly every girl I've met is in a relationship**, so I'm not sure how many single girls are in the city."

Q "**Unfortunately, the best places to meet people are usually bars**, but depending on what you're into, sporting or cultural events are just as good."

Q "The singles scene in Pittsburgh is horrible. **No one here is single!**"

Q "It can be somewhat difficult to meet people in the same age group in Pittsburgh. The best places to meet young people are **gyms, yoga studios, sporting events, classes, coffee shops**, and, of course, bars."

Q "It's not difficult—people are just superficial. Guys want the girl that is in the beer commercial, girls want guys that are rich. **It's more of a national problem than a city one**."

Q "I think it is **easy to meet people if you go out**."

Q "Because Pittsburgh has a huge college scene, there are always new people milling around. **Check out the happy hours to meet young professionals**."

Q "If you want to meet quality people **join a club or organization and stay out of the bars**. If you do go to the bars, make sure you check for wedding or engagement rings (just because somebody is young doesn't mean they aren't married)."

Q "The dating scene is pretty good. **All the girls are willing to talk to you if you're not a creep**. I've done tons and tons and tons of dating—so much dating that it's turned into a second job, except I'm not getting paid and I lose a lot of money."

Q "Many of the people who stay in Pittsburgh **grew up here and have an established base group of friends**—and therefore aren't out cruising to meet new friends. You will meet people if you stick with it, but I would recommend joining a group or club, not by going to bars."

The Urban Guru Take On...
Dating & Social Life

Take a look at some of the polls ranking the best U.S. cities for singles, and you'll see that Pittsburgh regularly makes the list—although it's usually in the bottom half. A recent *Forbes* magazine survey rated Pittsburgh 28th out of 40 major metropolitan areas based on each city's singles, nightlife, coolness, culture, job growth, online dating, and cost of living. Based on the number of singles alone, Pittsburgh ranks 21st. Despite the many great dating spots and cultural attractions it has to offer, Pittsburgh's dating scene tends to suffer for several reasons, including the dependence on bars as social hubs and the age of the population—only 25 percent of residents are between ages 20 and 35.

While it may require extra work to find romance in the city, young professionals should have no trouble finding friends with common interests—besides an interest in drinking. Museums, art galleries, and sporting events are all great places to both meet new people and socialize with the ones you already know. There are also several organizations that promote social interaction and networking among young Pittsburghers, including Pittsburgh Urban Magnet Program (PUMP) and Pittsburgh Young Professionals (PYP).

B

The Urban Guru® Grade on
Dating & Social Life: B

A high grade in Dating & Social Life indicates that the singles are attractive, smart, friendly, and engaging, and that there is a decent ratio of men to women. Other factors include ease of meeting new people and the vitality of the social scene in general.

Diversity

The Lowdown On...
Diversity

African American:
29%

Native American:
Less than 1%

Asian American:
4%

White:
64%

Hispanic:
1%

Foreign-Born:
6%

Multi-Racial:
2%

➜

www.collegeprowler.com/urbanguru

Diversity Resources:

Alternative Lifestyles
www.gaypittsburgh.com
www.glccpgh.org
www.outinpittsburgh.com

Minorities
www.aaccwp.com
www.county.allegheny.pa.us/
mwdbe
www.diversecitypittsburgh.org
www.pmahcc.org
www.paaypa.org
www.thesoulpitt.com
www.wbninc.com

Politics
allegheny.mygopsite.com
palwv.org
www.youngdemsallegheny.com

Religious Resources:

Christian/Catholic
www.avaoc.org
www.diopitt.org
www.pittsburgh.goarch.org
www.usachurch.com

Islamic
www.icp-pgh.org
www.islamicvalley.com

Jewish
www.jewishpittsburgh.org
www.jccpgh.org
www.ujfpittsburgh.org

Other
www.pittsburghbuddhist
center.org
www.pittsburghindia.com
www.prairiewindzen.org/zcp

Minority Organizations

African American Chamber of Commerce of Western Pennsylvania, August Wilson Center for African American Culture, Filipino American Association of Pittsburgh, Homer S. Brown Law Association, The Hispanic Center, Islamic Center of Pittsburgh, Minority Professional Network, National Association of Asian American Professionals (NAAAP) Pittsburgh, National Black MBA Association Pittsburgh, Pennsylvania National Organization for Women, Pittsburgh Metropolitan Area Hispanic Chamber of Commerce, Pittsburgh Regional Minority Purchasing Council, Pittsburgh Turkish American Association, Serb National Federation, Urban League of Greater Pittsburgh, Women and Girls Foundation of Southwest Pennsylvania, ZOA Pittsburgh

Political Activity

Just like it is in any area, there are some people who are involved in politics and others who don't care at all. Young Pittsburghers generally seem to be in touch with politics, and many get involved. The city is heavily Democratic, even more so among the young professionals here.

Gay Pride

The majority of Pittsburghers are accepting of alternative lifestyles, but there are some older residents who still have a 1950s mindset and may not be as open. The gay atmosphere here is smaller than it is in larger cities, but it's pretty good. There are several gay bars in the city, generally on Ellsworth Avenue in Shadyside or Liberty Avenue downtown. The Gay & Lesbian Community Center of Pittsburgh (*www.glccpgh.org*) hosts regular events, including the annual Pride Week, and the The Pittsburgh Lesbian and Gay Film Society, which has been around for 23 years, holds an annual film festival. Also check out the local GLBT publication, *Pittsburgh's Out* (*www.outpub.com*).

Economic Status

Pittsburgh is mostly middle class due to its blue-collar past, but that is changing. There are several luxury condos and lofts being built here and people are actually buying them, which shows that the economic landscape of Pittsburgh is changing.

Most Common Religions

Catholic, Christian, Jewish (mainly in Squirrel Hill)

Locals Speak Out On...
Diversity

> **"Pittsburgh is mostly white and working-class, but there is a significant African American population, with several historical black neighborhoods."**

Q "In terms of racial diversity, there's not much, but **I don't think there is a stereotypical Pittsburgher** in terms of political views or economic status. Pittsburghers as a whole don't care about anyone's sex life. What would bother them is someone being loud or showy about it."

Q "Pittsburgh is very diverse, and many young people are politically active. **The gay atmosphere is very open here in Pittsburgh**, and everyone is very accepted."

Q "Oakland, Shadyside, and Squirrel Hill probably have the **largest concentrations of Asian residents**."

Q "Pittsburgh is **diverse but highly segregated**."

Q "The gay bars and coffee shops are few and far between, but there are a **lot of groups that one can join to be a part of GLBT community**. People seem pretty open to it."

Q "Frankly, it's **not terribly diverse, but it's more so among young people**. Unfortunately, this is a city with a lot of senior citizens who tend to cling to their prejudices."

Q "Pittsburgh is pretty diverse and accepting of alternative lifestyles, and **young Pittsburghers are politically active**."

Q "It feels like **Shadyside, Squirrel Hill, and Oakland are bubbles of students and more diverse individuals**. Once you step out into East Liberty or other areas, it feels like the cultural diversity drops. In terms of alternative lifestyles, there's a high tolerance from my perspective, especially in Shadyside and the Ellsworth Avenue area."

Q "**The diversity here is horrible**—I'd say it's one of the worst in the country. How many black people do you work with? How many are in management?"

Q "**Pittsburgh is becoming more diverse with the years**. I think young Pittsburghers are very active and politically involved. There is a good gay atmosphere, people are very open, and I haven't seen discrimination in that sense."

Q "It seems like there are a lot of politically active people, which is great. **There seems to be a lot of gay bars**, which is good, but 'yinzers' need to be a little more open-minded and keep their mouths shut."

Q "In general, Pittsburghers are very tolerant of personal lifestyle choices, but there are a lot of bigots and 'good old boys' out there, so **it's not all flowers and sunshine**."

Q "There truly is not enough diversity at all. **We have terribly small Latino and Asian communities**, and everyone is a Democrat. Young Pittsburghers are only as active as pulling the 'D' lever. I'm tolerant of other lifestyles, and I think that most are—or they at least should be."

Q "Pittsburgh has a small but pretty good gay scene from what I've heard. Tolerance of homosexuals varies on location within the city. I wouldn't say Pittsburgh is an openly gay-friendly city, but **I've never heard of any harassment of gay people here**, either. Indifference is probably the best way to describe it."

Q "The population is **very diverse since there are a lot of universities in the area**. There are many racial, political, and economic clubs and groups."

Q "**It is overwhelmingly Catholic here, but there is a large Jewish population in Squirrel Hill**. Pittsburgh has a working-class feel to it, and most people here are solidly middle class."

Q "**The gay atmosphere is not very vibrant,** and people are not very tolerant."

Q "It's very Democratic here, and **there's a large diversity in terms of people's wealth**."

Q "Outside of the Steelers players, **there don't seem to be many black role models for teenagers**. Diversity is not a strength of the city."

Q "Pittsburgh is a black and white city. **There are some Asians and Indians, and there is a small Hispanic population** that is growing. You'll find the most diversity in Oakland, Shadyside, and Squirrel Hill, especially near the universities."

Q "I would say **it is pretty diverse for a small city**. It could be a lot worse."

Q "The diversity scene depends on where you are in Pittsburgh. Carnegie Mellon University has a lot of Asians, but other college campuses here are mainly white. Local **Pittsburghers tend to be a mix of white and black**, but there's not much variety other than that."

Q "I think **there is a good gay atmosphere here**, and most people are pretty tolerant to alternative lifestyles."

Q "**It can be diverse if you go looking for it**. Carnegie Mellon has lots of diverse students."

The Urban Guru Take On...
Diversity

Diversity in Pittsburgh basically means two races: white and black, with very low representation of Hispanics, Asians, and other races. One of the most diverse neighborhoods is Oakland, mostly due to its large student population from Carnegie Mellon and the University of Pittsburgh. The city is very rich in European culture, and you will find Deutschtown in the North Side, Little Italy (Bloomfield), and Polish Hill. In terms of religion, Pittsburgh has a large but declining Catholic population. Squirrel Hill is the center of the Jewish community in Pittsburgh, and you'll find numerous synagogues and Jewish restaurants, as well as the Jewish Community Center here. When it comes to politics, Pittsburgh is mainly Democratic. In fact, every mayor since 1933 has been a Democrat, and in 2008, there were twice as many registered Democrats in Allegheny County as there were Republicans.

Once home to smoke-filled skies and huge steel mills, the city is now home to corporate headquarters and one of the top health care providers in the country, which is reflected in Pittsburghers' economic status. Many are heavily rooted in the middle class, but there is a much wider range in terms of wealth and economic status now than ever before. Overall, the people of Pittsburgh are generally accepting of others and their lifestyle choices.

The Urban Guru® Grade on

Diversity: C+

A high grade in Diversity indicates that ethnic minorities have a notable presence in the city and that residents of different economic backgrounds, religious beliefs, and sexual preferences are well-represented.

Transportation & Parking

The Lowdown On...

Transportation & Parking

Commuters (Metro Area):

Drive Alone:	56%	(78%)
Public Transit:	19%	(5%)
Walk:	12%	(4%)
Carpool:	9%	(10%)
Work at Home:	3%	(3%)
Other Means:	1%	(<1%)

Mean Commute Time:

22.4 minutes
(National Avg.: 25.5 minutes)

Residential Parking Permits:

Not all residential streets fall into a parking permit area, but if yours does, rates are as follows:

One Year:	$20 per vehicle
Six Months:	$10 per vehicle
Visitor's Pass:	$1 per vehicle

Average Garage Rates:

Day Lease – $200–$275/month
Night Lease – $100/month
All-Day Parking – $10–$15

Common Parking Fines:

Expired Meter: $10–$16

No Permit: $25

Handicapped Zone: $100

Parking Office:

Pittsburgh Parking Authority

232 Boulevard of the Allies

(412) 560-PARK

www.city.pittsburgh.pa.us/ pghparkingauthority

The Parking Authority Web site provides maps of garage locations and their rates, as well as info on purchasing parking permits.

Ways to Get Around Town:

Public Transportation

Port Authority of Allegheny County

(412) 442-2000

www.portauthority.org

Average Bus Fare: $2
Transfers: $0.50

Port Authority operates all public buses in Allegheny County, as well as the inclines and the "T," a 25-mile light-rail system with two routes that run from Downtown to the South Hills. Schedules and fare information are available from the port authority's Web site.

Taxis

Classy Cab
(412) 322-5080

Eagle Cab
(412) 765-1555

People's Cab
(412) 441-3200

Yellow Cab
(412) 321-8100

Car Rentals

Alamo
Local: (412) 472-5060
National: (800) 462-5266
www.alamo.com

Avis – 11 area locations
Local: (412) 472-5200
National: (800) 331-1212
www.avis.com

Budget – 5 area locations
Local: (412) 472-5252
National: (800) 527-0700
www.budget.com

Dollar – 2 area locations
Local: (866) 434-2226
National: (800) 800-3665
www.dollarrentalcar.com

Enterprise – 29 area locations
Local: (412) 472-3490
National: (800) 261-7331
www.enterprise.com

Hertz – 10 area locations
Local: (412) 472-5955
National: (800) 654-3131
www.hertz.com

National
Local: (412) 472-5045
National: (800) 654-3001
www.nationalcar.com

Thrifty – 2 area locations
Local: (412) 472-5288
National: (800) 847-4389
www.thrifty.com

Best Ways to Get Around Town

Bike

Drive

Public Transportation

Walk

Ways to Get Out of Town:

Airport

Pittsburgh International Airport

(412) 472-3525

www.pitairport.com

Pittsburgh International Airport is located off Route 60 in Moon Township, west of the city.

Airlines serving Pittsburgh

Air Canada
(888) 247-2262
www.aircanada.com

AirTran Airways
(800) 247-8726
www.airtran.com

American Airlines
(800) 433-7300
www.aa.com

Continental
(800) 523-3273
www.continental.com

Delta
(800) 221-1212
www.delta.com

Jet Blue
(800) 538-2583
www.jetblue.com

Midwest Airlines
(800) 452-2022
www.midwestairlines.com

(Airlines, continued)

Northwest
(800) 225-2525
www.nwa.com

Southwest Airlines
(800) 435-9792
www.southwest.com

United
(800) 241-6522
www.united.com

US Airways
(800) 428-4322
www.usairways.com

USA3000
(877) 872-3000
www.usa3000.com

How to Get to the Airport

Take I-279 South, following signs for the Airport/Route 60.

Catch the 28X Airport Flyer.

Amtrak

Pittsburgh Amtrak Train Station

1100 Liberty Ave.

(412) 471-6172

www.amtrak.com

Greyhound

Pittsburgh Greyhound Trailways Bus Terminal

900 2nd Ave.

(412) 392-6513

www.greyhound.com

Did You Know?

There are **about 446 bridges in Pittsburgh**, earning the city one of its nicknames: City of Bridges. Although this is impressive, there is controversy over which city can claim to have the most bridges due to inconsistencies in defining a "bridge."

Pittsburgh features more than 700 public staircases. That is **more stairs than any other city in the nation, by far**—the first runner-up is Cincinnati with a mere 400!

Handy Pittsburgh Travel Tips

Carpool Tunnel Syndrome
Coming into Pittsburgh from the east, west, or south will usually require going through a tunnel. These tunnels (especially the Squirrel Hill Tunnel on I-376) are notorious for traffic congestion, so plan accordingly.

Fringe Benefits
The parking garages run by the Parking Authority aren't prohibitively expensive, but if you're looking for a more cost-effective commute downtown, try parking in one of the fringe lots in the Strip District or the North Shore. Many of these lots let you park all day for under $10.

Navigation Woes
Map out your driving routes thoroughly! Most Pittsburgh streets are very narrow, two-way streets often become one-way streets without warning, and the rivers and hills cut the city into odd shapes so that there is generally no easy "grid" to follow. Driving here is not for the faint of heart.

Parkway Prowess
Pittsburgh's major interstate arteries, referred to as "parkways," are each named for the region they serve. The Parkway East refers to I-376, which stretches eastward toward Monroeville, the Parkway West refers to I-279 as it heads west to the airport, and the Parkway North, also I-279, runs north to Cranberry.

Pedal Power

Pittsburgh's narrow streets and rolling hills have made it a pretty uninviting city for bicycle travel, but biking is slowly becoming more and more popular as transportation, and new bike lanes are popping up all over the city. Check out Bike Pittsburgh at *bike-pgh.org* for biking news and help with planning your route.

Pittsburghers Have the "Left of Way"

One of Pittsburgh's more controversial driving habits is a tradition known as the "Pittsburgh Left." Often, a driver waiting to turn left at an intersection will immediately pull out across the oncoming lane as soon as the light turns green instead of yielding to the straight-bearing traffic—usually without even waiting to be waved on by the driver in the opposing lane. This move isn't necessarily exclusive to Pittsburgh, but the city's constricted streets mean very few left-turn lanes and left-turn-signal lights, and this has made the Pittsburgh Left a widely-accepted part of the Pittsburgh driving experience. That fact doesn't make it any less illegal, however.

Put Your Hand Down

People don't hail taxis in Pittsburgh. It's sometimes possible to flag one down out of desperation when the bars are letting out in the popular nightlife hubs. Your best bet is to either call ahead or just take the bus.

Remember "Roy G. Biv"

Pittsburgh has no interstate beltway surrounding the city. Instead, the various neighborhoods are linked by the Belt Route System—a series of concentric loops circling the city. The belts are marked according to the colors of the rainbow, beginning with the Red Belt on the city's outskirts and ending with the Purple Belt which circles the heart of Downtown.

Street signs directing drivers to common destinations also follow their own color scheme known as the Wayfinder System—as if the Belt Routes weren't confusing enough. This breaks down the city into five regions and assigns a different color to each. Signs directing drivers to downtown locations are magenta, North Side uses light blue, South Side uses green, the East End uses orange, and the Strip District's are brownish-gold. Go to *www.routemarkers.com/usa/Pennsylvania/Wayfinder* for more info.

Locals Speak Out On...
Transportation & Parking

> "The bus sometimes doesn't show up on time, but at least there is a bus. The T is almost pointless unless you are just getting from one point to the next downtown."

Q "**Pittsburgh's public transportation is not very good compared to other cities**. The buses don't run very frequently on many of the routes and are often very crowded. I would like to use it more regularly, but I find it so much of a hassle that I avoid it whenever possible."

Q "Traffic is sometimes **fairly heavy at rush hour**, particularly when you have to travel through one or more of the tunnels, which seem to be a clogging point. Also, travel in the South Hills is sometimes slower because there just aren't any good roads to get from point A to point B."

Q "The bus system is OK, but why is there is no light rail transportation from Shadyside, Squirrel Hill, or Oakland to Downtown? **Instead, we are building a $1 billion tunnel under the river**."

Q "It's reliable, for the most part. **The further away from the city you go, the less often buses come there**."

Q "**Avoid all tunnels during rush hour, home sporting events, and major concerts**. If they are performing construction on the tunnel, avoid it at all costs at any time of day or night."

Q "I use public transportation once a week. It is reliable, but **prices are rising**."

Q "Public transportation is OK, but I rarely use it. **It is safe and available in all areas of the city**, but it's sometimes not on time."

Q "The public transportation is great. The bus schedule is reliable, and **if you know the schedule, the bus will be there**. It is safe."

Q "It sucks! Actually, I take that back. There are plenty of options, but it is run so poorly that they can't seem to get out of their own way. Also, **it is impossible to find a cab**, leading you to often drive when you really shouldn't."

Q "I commute about 40 minutes each way each day. I commute from the city to the suburbs. **It is a relaxing drive, and I almost never hit traffic.**"

Q "Traffic from 7 a.m. to 8 a.m. is pretty bad. Route 28 from around the Highland Park Bridge into the city gets backed up. **Downtown is very expensive to park, but it's usually easy to find a garage** if you get into town before 9 a.m. The Strip District has a few $5-a-day lots and a shuttle into town, so it's a good cheaper option."

Q "It's bad to drive any time in the winter. **A little bit of snow and people can't drive**! Also, the little bit of snow makes it hard to see the enormous pot holes that have developed because PennDot and Public Works are bureaucratic disasters."

Q "It's relatively easy to use the bus, but it doesn't always feel safe. **The 28X to the airport is reliable**."

Q "**The commute is nothing compared to other cities**. People will complain, but they have nothing to compare it to. From someone who has lived in other cities, our commute is easy!"

Q "**Worst transportation system in the country**. It is straight out of a '60s movie. I saw local buses in a small underdeveloped town in China 12 years ago with a better system than Pittsburgh's. It does not make sense to me that you pay when you get off."

Q "It's worst during rush hour or rainy days. Pittsburghers can't drive, and **they don't know how to work the merge point**. With all the construction going on in the city, Pittsburghers need to learn this."

Q "Transportation is limited to buses mostly. If you are downtown, **you can use the subway for three stops**."

Q "Port Authority is good, and for the most part, reliable. **My biggest complaint is that it doesn't operate after club hours**."

Q "The worst place to drive is 376 eastbound to the turnpike between 2 p.m. and 6 p.m. **Why can't people maintain their speed through a tunnel**?"

Q "It's good within the city and in areas like Oakland, South Side, and Shadyside. **The T is good for people who live in the South Hills**. Otherwise, the public transportation isn't so great if you live a bit farther out."

Q "**Route 28 is horrible**! The traffic is bad in the morning and afternoon. If you have other options, use them!"

Q "For those within the city limits, the public transportation is great. Sometimes buses and trolleys come when they want, but it's generally very safe and pretty reliable. For those who live in the suburbs, **budget and service cuts have left people with few options to get into the city**."

Q "**The best parking is just outside downtown** in the Strip District or at Heinz Field."

Q "I drive 15 to 20 minutes from 10 miles outside the city to Downtown. **I think my commute is better than it would be in any other city**."

Q "The only way I can get around is by bus. However, the bus is **extremely infrequent and unreliable** in terms of schedules, so a five-minute bus ride will turn into 45 minutes when you include waiting around for the bus."

Q "It's pretty good. **I take a bus daily**."

Q "Commutes here are short, and traffic is generally light compared to other cities. Exceptions include commuting from the south or east, where the highways pass through tunnels. **Pittsburghers can't seem to maintain their speed through tunnels**. During non-rush hour times, everything in Pittsburgh is 20 minutes away or less."

Q "I used to use the bus. **It is reliable and accessible, but they started cutting down on schedules**."

Q "Well, when you cut routes, it's not good. We need to advertise the crap out of PAT because **not enough people take it**. It takes me an hour to get from Lebanon Church Road to 10th Street in the South Side just because everyone feels the need to drive through there."

Q "My commute is about 40 minutes on a normal weekday. It is a headache, especially in the winter, and construction is a factor throughout the spring, summer, and fall. Garages make parking fairly simple within the city, but **finding on-street parking can be more difficult**. Currently public transportation is very limited. It would be great if they would expand and offer services to a wider area."

Q "In busy areas of the city like the South Side local residents often place cones along the curb to save their parking spaces. **Do not move these to park** in the space unless you want your windows broken or tires slashed."

The Urban Guru Take On...
Transportation & Parking

Getting around in Pittsburgh is a unique experience to put it lightly. It's a city whose greatest expansion took place in pre-automobile days, and it shows. Narrow city streets tend to be major commuter routes, and the city layout itself is a haphazard tangle of rapidly changing one-way streets. You may consider opting for public transportation until you get your bearings—though your options will generally be limited to the buses, as taxi cabs aren't widely available, and the subway system currently only travels between Downtown and the South Hills. If Pittsburgh has one saving grace in the transportation department, it's that traffic is fairly light compared to larger cities. Once you manage to figure out where you're going, you'll find yourself getting there pretty quickly. Just be aware that the city's many tunnels and bridges are choke points, and they can increase your commute time dramatically, especially during rush hours.

Parking in the city can range from easy to impossible. Parking downtown is generally a breeze because of the abundance of parking garages, but finding parking in popular neighborhoods like Shadyside, the South Side, and the Strip District is often dependent on pure luck and parallel parking skills. Assume that parking will be difficult and leave yourself enough time to make a few trips around the block.

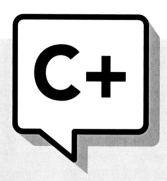

The Urban Guru® Grade on
Transportation & Parking: C+

A high grade for Transportation & Parking indicates that public buses, cabs, and rental cars are available and affordable. Other determining factors include availability of parking, traffic levels, proximity to an airport, and the necessity of transportation.

Report Card Summary

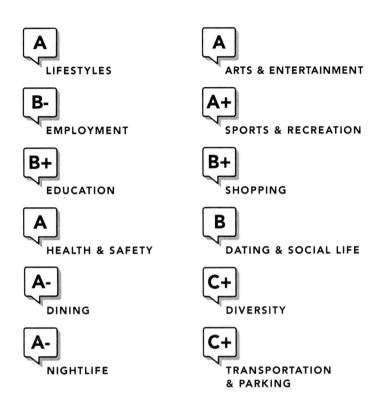

A LIFESTYLES

B- EMPLOYMENT

B+ EDUCATION

A HEALTH & SAFETY

A- DINING

A- NIGHTLIFE

A ARTS & ENTERTAINMENT

A+ SPORTS & RECREATION

B+ SHOPPING

B DATING & SOCIAL LIFE

C+ DIVERSITY

C+ TRANSPORTATION & PARKING

Overall Experience

Locals Speak Out On...
Overall Experience

> "It is a great city to live in comfortably. There are many events and sites to experience, and everything can fit comfortably into a budget. After living here for four years, I've found it is sometimes difficult to meet people, so it can be tempting to move."

"On a scale of 1 to 10 (with 1 being the worst experience ever and 10 being the best), I'd rate Pittsburgh as an 8. I hate the roads and Pittsburgh drivers, and I hate finding parking, but I love everything else! So the two things I hate are made up for by all the things I love. Pittsburgh has a lot to offer—**there's something for everyone**. I've been here for more than two years, and currently, I am planning on staying in Pittsburgh. We'll see."

www.collegeprowler.com/urbanguru

Q "I love Pittsburgh because it's home. It is a friendly town, and although there are fluky things aplenty, **there is much more to love than to hate**. I've lived here my whole life except for one year I spent in Palm Beach, Fla., but two months after I left, I was ready to come home. Although I would love to have a home somewhere else in the future, I will always come home to Pittsburgh."

Q "Pittsburgh is a town that I'd like to hug and choke at the same time. There are so many great things about it, but **it's provincial and very slow moving**."

Q "**I love that Pittsburghers love Pittsburgh** whether they've lived here their entire lives or only for a short while. Running into someone at a bar wearing a Steelers shirt hundreds or thousands of miles from home can forge an instant friendship before you say a word. There's also that unspoken rule that a Pittsburgher can trash talk any of the local athletes up and down without question, but if a non-Pittsburgher says a word about Big Ben or Sid the Kid, they are truly taking their lives into their own hands."

Q "It's a good city to live in. A lot of people that live here stay here and are loyal to the city, and it has a lot to offer. Unfortunately, **I've always been here and probably always will**. I say unfortunately not because Pittsburgh is a bad place to live but because there is so much more world out there to see."

Q "It's OK, but to be honest, I preferred visiting when I lived elsewhere. I can say that it is a great place to say you are from and to go home and visit, but **I don't think I will be living here in a couple years**."

Q "I like Pittsburgh because I grew up around here. It's **showing signs of revitalizing itself** into an exciting and fun place to be. I lived here until I was 18, when I moved away for school, and didn't return until I was 27. I've been back for almost two years now, and I don't plan on leaving anytime soon."

Q "I am absolutely in love with Pittsburgh. **I love the sunrise over the city when I drive through the Fort Pitt Tunnel** in the morning and all the opportunities and events in the city. I hate the parking, traffic, inspection/emissions laws, and the massive amount of taxes I pay."

Q "I think Pittsburgh is a great city that has really developed over the past decade. The cost of living is affordable, there are job opportunities, and it is a bigger city with a small-town atmosphere. Everyone is approachable and generally willing to help, and I have made strong connections in the 'Burgh, **both professional relationships and personal friendships**, that I think will last for a long time to come."

Q "I like it here, but I want to get out. I've been here for four years, and **it's not as good as back home** in Maryland. I'm going to move away after I graduate this year."

Q "Pittsburgh is probably a love-it-or-hate-it city. I think it would be hard to live here if you had no interest whatsoever in spectator sports. That said, I think it's possible to find just about any kind of person, group, or place to fit in somewhere. There is a ton of stuff to do here, though you may have to look a bit harder than you would in New York City. I think **Pittsburgh is a good place for someone who is unpretentious**, someone who is not overly concerned about impressing other people, and someone who, above all, likes to have fun. I will never leave Pittsburgh voluntarily."

Q "Pittsburgh does not have the best reputation as a city to people outside of this area, but don't worry. **It's a city that grows on you**."

Q "I love the city because it is more unique than my hometown. I just wish the city would listen to its concerned residents that are questioning their personal safety in their own neighborhoods. **We need to desaturate the South Side of bars and alcohol** and bring in more unique shops that would draw a lot of tourists, especially families."

Q "Overall, I love it here, but I'm only staying while I'm in grad school. I wouldn't want to live here—there's not enough ethnic diversity for me outside of the academic environment. And it is a small town—**you run into people you know everywhere**, which can have its perks, but it's too small of a town for me. I'll stay here for another year or so until I graduate, and after that, I'm looking to move to a coast or other big city."

Q "I've lived here my whole life, and I've loved it, but if the job market doesn't get better, **I may be forced to leave**."

Q "**I used to hate Pittsburgh, but now I love it**. It is a beautiful city, and there is plenty to do. I hate that they sometimes don't salt the roads for several days during the winter, though. In all, the city is very organized and friendly, and I plan to stay in Pittsburgh for the next five years."

Q "I love the city. It's a great small city, it's relatively clean, there is a lot to do, and the people are really nice. I just wish the Pirates would start winning. I have lived here all but four years of my life, when I lived in Hartford, Conn. **Pittsburgh beats Hartford by a mile**."

Q "I love this city. **I could never imagine leaving here**. I like the city life a lot. I have lived here for three years, and I will be staying for the rest of my life."

Q "It's home, and I like it a lot. **I'll be here for the long haul**."

Q "Pittsburgh's a great city for people who like a city atmosphere without being overwhelmed. I've lived here for about a year and a half, and I really like it. I grew up in upstate New York and lived in some craptastic smaller cities. Pittsburgh is a bigger city with plenty of things going on, but it's not overwhelming, and **the best part is the super-low cost of living**. Everything is cheaper here than it was in New York, including gas, utilities, and taxes. Plus, we were able to buy a house even though I took a pay cut here."

Q "I love the affordable theatre and symphony tickets, the hills, and the bridges. **I hate the gray skies and the resistance to political change.**"

Q "I love Pittsburgh! It's a beautiful city, there's plenty to do, and the people are generally friendly. **Of course, winter lasts too long**, but it's worth it when spring comes and the city is in bloom! I've lived in the area my entire life and in the city for about five years, and I think we'll be here for a long time."

Q "I've lived here for 10 years. The only other place I've lived was very rural, so Pittsburgh is very different. I thought I wouldn't like it, but once I got past the 'culture shock' of living in a city, I really started to love Pittsburgh. I'm sure I'll be living in Pittsburgh for a long time. My husband grew up in Pittsburgh, and **people who grew up in Pittsburgh seem to never leave**!"

Q "I love Pittsburgh. I always go back and visit, and it is a relatively cheap getaway. Since I went to college in the city, I have such nostalgic memories that visiting always puts me in a good mood. **As long as you can live with the frequent cloudy days, it is a great city.**"

Q "My favorite part of Pittsburgh is that the Yinzers are real people who love sports and having fun. Plus, **it isn't a materialistic city**. Bars rarely have a dress code more than a collared shirt, and you don't have to pay a lot for a drink. It's a big small town—after living here for a short time you feel like part of the neighborhood."

Q "Overall, I love living in Pittsburgh. The people tend to be down-to-earth and real, and the city has a strong character. **I love the traditions and the different neighborhoods,** and I especially love that we enjoy four distinct seasons— even if winter can be a drag sometimes!

The Urban Guru Take On...
Overall Experience

Pittsburgh is a great city with something for everyone. If you prefer quiet neighborhoods, there are plenty to choose from—and not just in the suburbs! If you thrive on the hustle and bustle of city life, there are plenty of places where you'll fit right in, especially Oakland, the Strip District, or Downtown. Sports fanatics will absolutely love it here, and nature lovers will feel right at home with several large parks throughout the city and many state parks within a short drive. People with children, or anyone thinking of having children, will enjoy the city's many kid-friendly activities and venues. Love food? Pittsburgh has tons of great restaurants. And on top of that, Pittsburgh has an extremely low cost of living, friendly people, an excellent cultural district, some of the top school districts in the country, and world-class hospitals and health care systems.

Of course, Pittsburgh is not without its faults. Like any city in the Northeast, the weather can be very dreary at times, especially during the winter, but autumn is gorgeous when the hillsides surrounding the city turn orange, red, and yellow. The transportation system isn't the best, and you might have trouble finding affordable nonstop flights out of the airport—especially to West Coast destinations, which is definitely a pain if you're a frequent flyer. In terms of jobs, the market can be a bit tough here. Creative jobs can be scarce, but Pittsburgh is home to several Fortune 500 companies, and there are plenty of opportunities in health care, insurance, and education. Start-up businesses are also common. Pittsburgh may not be a perfect city, but with all it has going for it, Pittsburgh could be perfect for you—so what are you waiting for?

The Inside Scoop

The Lowdown On...
The Inside Scoop

Pittsburgh Slang:

Also known as "Pittsburghese," the region's dialect is often the result of being in too much of a hurry to enunciate properly. Love it or hate it, Pittsburghese is a way of life for many.

Aht – Out

Crick – Creek

Com'ere – Come here

Dahntahn – Downtown

Dippy Egg – Fried egg with yolk intact for dipping

G'ahead – Go ahead

Giant Iggle – Local supermarket chain Giant Eagle

Gumband – Rubber band

Hoagie – Submarine sandwich

Jagger – Thorn or anything pointy (also: Jaggerbush)

Jag or Jagoff – A stupid jerk

The Mon – Shortened name for the Monongahela River

N'at – And that

Nebby – Nosy

Pixburgh – How some locals pronounce Pittsburgh

Pop – Soda

Redd up – Clean or tidy up

Slippy – Slippery

Tubes – Tunnels, of which there are several in Pittsburgh

Worsh – Wash

Y'inz – Plural "you"

Yinzer – A generally negative name for a stereotypical Pittsburgher

Things I Wish I Knew Before Coming to Pittsburgh

- Pittsburgh is very neighborhood-oriented. Definitely walk around a bunch of neighborhoods to find out which one fits you best—where you live can really impact your experience.

- Enjoy the unique culture—there's a lot to appreciate in the little corners of neighborhoods.

- Bring a lot of winter clothes!

- Consider the low cost of living and weigh that against any downsides to the city. The airport is not that convenient, but you can still travel to other places easily. Although you can see the entire city in a few years, it's about the people you meet and become close to.

- Driving around Pittsburgh can be very confusing. There are a lot of places where "you can't get there from here." Think about getting GPS.

- Landlords can be shady—make sure you know what you're getting into before you sign a lease.

- Income taxes within the city limits are high—generally equal to or greater than the state tax rate—and property taxes can be substantial depending on your school district and home value.

- Watch the WQED Pittsburgh history series! There is so much cool stuff to learn about this area.

- Keep an open mind. Pittsburgh has a lot to offer, but comparing it to New York or Los Angeles is like comparing apples and oranges.

- Pittsburgh was rated as the "Most Livable City" by Places Rated Almanac in 2007.

Pittsburgh Musts

- Take an incline ride up to **Mt. Washington** to enjoy the view from one of many overlooks along Grandview Avenue.

- Spend a Saturday walking one of the **popular shopping districts** in Shadyside, Squirrel Hill, South Side, or the Strip.

- Tour **Phipps Conservatory** for a glimpse at some gorgeous plants and flowers, not to mention the beautiful architecture.

- Check out the **Carnegie Science Center** for some hands-on fun, a tour of a submarine, or an Omnimax movie.

- Enjoy a **Primanti's sandwich** at the original Strip location— it's especially good after a night of living it up at the Strip's bars and clubs.

- Go to a **Pirates game at PNC Park** if only to enjoy the view of the city from the stands.

- Watch the **Fourth of July fireworks** from Point State Park, Mt. Washington, or even better—from a boat on the river.

- Tailgate with the fans before a **Steelers home game**—but be sure you're wearing the right jersey.

- Jump on the **Gateway Clipper** or the Just Ducky tour for a quick history lesson and to see the city from the water.

- Visit **Penn Brewery** for a sampling of local brews and traditional German food—especially during Oktoberfest.

- Cool off at **Sandcastle on a summer day**, then drive over to enjoy Kennywood at night—tickets are discounted after 5 p.m.

- Convene with nature by visiting the **Pittsburgh Zoo & PPG Aquarium and the National Aviary** in one day. The zoo can easily be walked in under three hours, and the aviary is a short 10-minute drive away.

- Participate in a **Gallery Crawl**, a free quarterly showcase of art, music, food, and fun in Pittsburgh's Cultural District.

- Watch a free movie in one of Pittsburgh's parks through the Citiparks **Cinema in the Parks** program, which runs from June to August.

- Join the leagues of the undead at one of Pittsburgh's record-setting **zombie walks at the Monroeville Mall**, where George Romero's classic "Dawn of the Dead" was filmed in 1978.

Did You Know?

The View from the Top

- *Forbes* magazine placed Pittsburgh among the Top 10 World's Cleanest Cities, **recognizing the city's transformation** from a primarily manufacturing economy to one based on health care, education, technology, and financial services.

- Pittsburgh ranks **seventh among the Top 10 Underrated U.S. Cities**. According to *ShermansTravel.com*, the city is recognized for its architecture, parks, and natural beauty.

- *Cooking Light* magazine listed Pittsburgh in its Top 20 Best Cities Awards based on **American cities that strive to eat smart, be fit, and live well**. Pittsburgh ranked 13th based on criteria that included healthfulness and exercise data, restaurant ratings, farmers' market listings, and parks and recreation data.

- *Bizjournals* ranked Pittsburgh **eighth of the nation's 50 largest markets on fun potential** because of the great shopping, culture, and sports opportunities in the area.

Pittsburgh Urban Legends

Birthplace of the Emoticon

Was the emoticon really invented by a Carnegie Mellon University professor? While Professor Scott Fahlman may have been the first to use a sideways smiley in an online format, the concept of using punctuation to portray emotions has been around for more than 40 years.

Brothel Laws

"More than X-number of women living together in a house constitutes a brothel, which is why there are no sorority houses in Pennsylvania." This urban legend is repeated on campuses nationwide, always with a different number, and it's false no matter how you cut it. The belief originated from zoning laws that once prohibited a certain number of non-family members, male or female, from living under one roof. A brothel is legally defined only by the activities that go on inside the building, not by who lives there.

Heinz 57

Heinz's famous catch phrase, "57 Varieties," was selected because the company sold exactly 57 different products. Unfortunately, this is just a myth—Heinz had more than 60 product varieties by the 1890s, when Henry Heinz came up with the slogan after seeing an ad for "21 styles of shoes" in New York City. The number 57 was chosen simply because the numbers 5 and 7 had significance to Heinz and his wife.

Trippy Pitcher

Pittsburgh Pirates pitcher Doc Ellis pitched a no-hitter in 1970 while under the influence of LSD. Ellis himself claims that he thought the Pirates were off that day, so he took some LSD only to discover later that not only were the Pirates playing a double-header that day but that he was scheduled to start the first game. Although there were no hits, Ellis' pitching was notably erratic—he walked eight batters and hit one.

Won't You Be My Sniper?

One prolific area urban legend is the false claim that Fred Rogers of *Mister Rogers' Neighborhood* had a violent criminal past. Variations of this myth include the idea that Rogers served as a sniper in Vietnam, both of which are false.

Pittsburgh Traditions

The Great Race
An annual Pittsburgh tradition presented by Highmark Blue
Cross Blue Shield in memory of late mayor Richard S. Caliguiri,
the Great Race attracts almost 10,000 participants each year.
Events include a 10K run, 5K run, 5K walk, wheelchair race,
and other competitions. Proceeds benefit the Richard S.
Caliguiri Amyloidosis Fund.

Hartwood Acres Celebration of Lights
This massive annual holiday light display covers more
than three miles and includes more than 400 displays that
revelers can enjoy from the comfort and warmth of their cars.
Donations benefit The Salvation Army's Project Bundle-Up, a
program that provides winter clothing to children and seniors.

Light-Up Night
Light-Up Night celebrates the official opening of the holiday
season the Friday before Thanksgiving. Festivities include the
unveiling of the Macy's Christmas displays, the arrival of Santa
Claus, and of course a fireworks extravaganza.

Pittsburgh Regatta & Fourth of July Fireworks
Pittsburgh's annual Independence Day celebration features
tons of free family friendly fun, including boat races, water
skiing entertainment, DJs, and live concerts, and culminates
with a giant fireworks display from Zambelli.

Pittsburgh Vintage Grand Prix
After 25 years, this event has grown from a single-day event
to a 10-day festival with car shows and cruises, formal galas,
and parades that culminates in a vintage car (pre-1965) race
through Schenley Park. Proceeds benefit the Autism Society of
Pittsburgh and the Allegheny Valley School.

St. Patrick's Day Parade
Pittsburghers don't normally need an excuse to start drinking
at 6 a.m., but it takes motivation to stand outside in the
freezing cold to watch bagpipes. This event is huge—one of
the biggest St. Patty's Day parades in the country. Follow the
party to Market Square afterward to get in touch with the Irish
in you and drink your fill of green beer.

(Traditions, continued)

Steelers Broadcasts—TV vs. Radio
It's a long-standing tradition for Steelers fans to watch game broadcasts with the TV volume turned down and the radio broadcast turned up.

Three Rivers Arts Festival
This two-week festival is held every June in Gateway Center Plaza and Point State Park downtown and features live music, art, jewelry, and food vendors. Get there on the first beautiful day or you might not get another chance—it's a running joke that it always rains for the Arts Festival.

Did You Know?

Pennsylvania Laws to Know:

- Fireworks are illegal in Pennsylvania, and vendors in other states **can get in trouble for selling fireworks to Pennsylvania residents**, even when the sale takes place in another state.

- In Pennsylvania, alcohol sales are controlled by the state. All wine and liquor must be purchased at a state Wine and Spirits store, and all beer purchases larger than a 12-pack must be made at a beer distributor. While there are no **alcohol sales at supermarkets or convenience stores**, many bars and restaurants will sell six-packs to go for inflated prices.

- Pennsylvania **blue laws prohibit hunting** and the sale of cars on Sundays, and alcohol sales are limited.

- Rumor has it that Pennsylvania has some really crazy laws, like the idea that it is **illegal to sleep outdoors on top of a refrigerator**, that it is illegal to use dynamite to catch fish, and that it is forbidden to bring a donkey onto a trolley in Pittsburgh, but it's hard to prove that these laws actually exist.

The Best & Worst

The Ten **BEST** Things About Pittsburgh

1 Low cost of living and affordable housing with all the big-city amenities and fun.

2 Sports! Pittsburgh fans are seriously dedicated to the Steelers, Penguins, and Pirates—win or lose.

3 Friendly locals and lots of young people make for a lively social scene.

4 Easy access to some of the best doctors and hospitals in the country.

5 Unique neighborhoods fit any personality—you could experience a new area every week for nearly two years!

6 Physical beauty, in both the skyline and the natural environment.

7 Variety of fun things to do, from river sports to amusement parks.

8 Rich history and cultural heritage are represented in the number of museums, art galleries, and other cultural sites.

(Ten Best, continued)

9 Great variety of excellent restaurants with reasonable prices and unique menus.

10 Environmental conscience—the city has the largest and most diverse collection of green buildings in the country.

The Ten WORST Things About Pittsburgh

1 Tunnel and bridge traffic. No one in Pittsburgh can seem to handle the concept of "maintain speed through tunnel."

2 It sometimes seems like the weather is always cloudy, rainy, or snowy.

3 Region is slow to embrace change. Pittsburgh is an urban island in the middle of a rural sea, so some outdated ideals still hold strong.

4 Public transportation becomes sparse further outside of the city, and timetables can be merely suggestions.

5 Construction! It is said that there are just two seasons in Pittsburgh: winter and construction.

6 What diversity? Outside of the educational communities, there isn't much racial diversity, especially from Asian, Latino, and Middle Eastern backgrounds.

7 Potholes are an unfortunate mainstay. Learn to dodge them for the sake of your rims and hubcaps.

8 While the financial and technology sectors thrive here, jobs can be difficult to find in creative fields.

9 Litter and rundown or abandoned buildings are common in some neighborhoods, though city leaders are working to combat urban blight.

10 Income taxes for city residents are as high as state taxes, and depending on what school district you live in, property taxes can be a big bite out of your income.

Events Calendar

Annual Events Calendar

January

Pittsburgh RV Show, Convention Center Downtown – *Early Jan.*

February

Pittsburgh Int'l Auto Show, Convention Center – *Mid-Feb.*

Winterfest at Seven Springs, Laurel Highlands – *Mid-Feb.*

March

Pittsburgh Home & Garden Show, Convention Center – *Early March*

St. Patrick's Day Parade, Downtown – *Mid-March*

Pittsburgh Jewish-Israeli Film Festival – *Late March*

April

Art All Night, Lawrenceville – *Late April*

May

Pittsburgh Wine Festival, Heinz Field – *Early May*

St. Nick's Greek Food Festival, Oakland – *Early May*

International Children's Festival, North Shore – *Mid-May*

Pittsburgh Race for the Cure, Schenley Park – *Mother's Day*

Silk Screen Asian American Film Festival – *Mid-May*

Pittsburgh Folk Festival, Convention Center – *May*

June

Pittsburgh Microbrewers Fest, Penn Brewery (North Side) – *Early June*

➜

(June, continued)

Three Rivers Arts Festival, Point State Park – *Early June*

Laurel Highlands Bluegrass Music Festival, Waterford – *Mid-June*

Pittsburgh Pride Week and PrideFest – *Mid-June*

WYEP Summer Music Festival, Schenley Plaza – *Late June*

Wings Over Pittsburgh Air Show, Moon Twp. – *June/July*

July

Big Butler Fair, Butler – *Early July*

Pittsburgh Three Rivers Regatta, Point State Park – *Early July*

Westmoreland Arts & Heritage Festival, Greensburg – *Early July*

Doo Dah Days, Lawrenceville – *Mid-July*

Pittsburgh Vintage Grand Prix, Schenley Park – *Mid-July*

Bedford County Fair, Bedford – *Late July*

Fayette County Fair, Dunbar – *Late July*

Pittsburgh Blues Festival, Hartwood Acres – *Late July*

August

Fort Armstrong Folk Festival, Kittanning – *Early August*

Festa Italiana, Vandergrift – *Mid-August*

Westmoreland Fair, Greensburg – *Mid-August*

Kickoff and Rib Festival, North Shore – *Late August*

Greater Pittsburgh Renaissance Festival, West Newton – *Late Aug./Early Sept.*

September

A Fair in the Park, Mellon Park (Point Breeze) – *Early Sept.*

Greater Pittsburgh Irish Festival, Homewood – *Early Sept.*

Pittsburgh Dragon Boat Festival, South Side – *Mid-Sept.*

Shadyside Arts Festival, Shadyside – *Mid-Sept.*

Little Italy Days, Bloomfield – *Late Sept.*

Penn Brewery Oktoberfest, North Side – *Late Sept.*

Penn's Colony Festival, Saxonburg – *Late Sept.*

October

Pittsburgh International Lesbian & Gay Film Festival – *Mid-Oct.*

November

Three Rivers Film Festival – *Early Nov.*

Light-Up Night Pittsburgh, Downtown – *Friday before Thanksgiving*

Celebrate the Season Parade, Downtown – *Saturday after Thanksgiving*

December

Celebration of Lights, Hartwood – *Mid-Nov.–Early Jan.*

First Night Pittsburgh, Downtown – *New Year's Eve*

Visiting

The Lowdown On...
Visiting

Hotel Information:

Hampton Inn & Suites Pittsburgh–Downtown

1247 Smallman St., Strip District

(412) 288-4350

www.hamptoninn.com

Nearby Attractions: Shops, restaurants, and bars in the Strip District

Price Range: $159–$239

What the Locals Say: "New and very nice."

Holiday Inn Express Hotel & Suites Pittsburgh–South Side

20 S. 10th St., South Side

(877) 863-4780

www.hiexpress.com

Nearby Attractions: Duquesne Incline, South Side bars and restaurants, SouthSide Works, Station Square

Price Range: $164–$243

What the Locals Say: "Close to Downtown, Station Square, and obviously everything in the South Side; good for the younger crowd."

➡

Marriott Pittsburgh City Center

112 Washington Pl., Downtown

(412) 471-4000

www.marriott.com

Nearby Attractions: Mellon Arena is across the street.

Price Range: $169–$289

What the Locals Say: "This is a good hotel if you're older or going to a Penguins game."

Omni William Penn Hotel

530 William Penn Pl., Downtown

(412) 281-7100

www.omniwilliampenn.com

Nearby Attractions: Cultural district, downtown restaurants and shopping, Heinz Field, Mellon Arena, PNC Park

Price Range: $199–$355

What the Locals Say: "Beautiful, old, and fancy, but expensive; good location in the middle of Downtown; great service."

The Priory Hotel

614 Pressley St., North Shore

(412) 231-3338

(866) 3PRIORY

www.thepriory.com

Nearby Attractions: Children's Museum, Heinz Field, PNC Park, The Warhol Museum

Price Range: $125–$230

What the Locals Say: "The service is awesome."

Renaissance Pittsburgh Hotel

107 6th St., Downtown

(412) 562-1200

(800) 468-3571

www.renaissancepittsburgh.com

Nearby Attractions: Cultural district, downtown restaurants and shopping, Heinz Field, Mellon Arena, PNC Park, The Warhol Museum

Price Range: $199–$399

What the Locals Say: "Beautiful lobby and décor; centrally located; historic building; my favorite hotel."

Shadyside Inn Suites

5405 Fifth Ave., Shadyside

(412) 441-4444

(800) 76-SUITE

www.shadysideinn.com

Nearby Attractions: Carnegie Mellon University, Carnegie Museum of Natural History, Phipps Conservatory, University of Pittsburgh, Walnut Street shopping

Price Range: $119–$189

What the Locals Say: "Location is great and everything you need is within walking distance; large, apartment-style rooms."

Sheraton Station Square

300 W. Station Square Dr. Station Square

(412) 261-2000

sheraton.com/stationsquare

(Sheraton, continued)

Nearby Attractions: Gateway Clipper, Duquesne and Monongahela inclines, Station Square shops and restaurants

Price Range: $239–$304

What the Locals Say: "Beautiful hotel; great view; nice, upscale location."

SpringHill Suites North Shore

223 Federal St., North Shore

(412) 323-9005

www.marriott.com

Nearby Attractions: Carnegie Science Center, downtown restaurants and shops, Heinz Field, PNC Park (shares a parking lot with the hotel)

Price Range: $179–$224

(Spring Hill Suites, continued)

What the Locals Say: "Best place to stay if you're going to a game; the suites are very clean and stylish."

Sunnyledge Boutique Hotel & Tea Room

5124 Fifth Ave., Shadyside

(412) 683-5014

www.sunnyledge.com

Nearby Attractions: Carnegie Mellon University, Carnegie Museums of Art and Natural History, Phipps Conservatory, University of Pittsburgh, Walnut Street shopping

Price Range: $189–$275

What the Locals Say: "Service is good; more unique than staying in standard chain hotel."

Did You Know?

Top Hotels to Stay at in Pittsburgh:

1. Renaissance Pittsburgh Hotel
2. Omni William Penn
3. Sheraton Station Square

Frommer's selected Pittsburgh as **one of the top 13 travel destinations for 2008** based on big city fun, rural relaxation, and physical vigor, not to mention the rich history and culture of the region. Pittsburgh was in good company, chosen among the likes of St. Lucia, Ecuador, and Morocco.

Day Trips from Pittsburgh

Cook Forest State Park

About two hours north of Pittsburgh is Cook Forest State Park (*www.cookforest.com*), a perfect place to spend the day hiking, fishing, canoeing, or river tubing. Turn your day trip into a weekend event, and bring a tent or stay at one of the two cabin areas here.

Fallingwater

Fallingwater, about 90 minutes from the city, is the house Frank Lloyd Wright built over a waterfall for Pittsburgh's Kaufmann family, founders of Kaufmann's Department Store, now part of Macy's. Completed in 1937, the house combines indoors with nature: a boulder hearth pokes through the living room, the sound of the waterfall can be heard throughout the house, and there are no panes in the windows to obstruct the view. Check out *www.fallingwater.org* for tour information.

Ohiopyle State Park

Outdoor enthusiasts will love this park, about an hour and a half south of Pittsburgh, because the recreational activities are nearly endless, including biking, camping, fishing, hiking, horseback riding, and winter sports like cross-country skiing, sledding, and snowmobiling. Adventure seekers will love Ohiopyle because of its whitewater rafting opportunities on the Lower Youghiogheny River and the natural waterslides in Meadow Run.

Presque Isle State Park

Pittsburgh is a good six or seven hours from any beaches on the coast, so the next best thing is Presque Isle—a sandy peninsula on Lake Erie. The park, about two hours north of Pittsburgh, has 13 beaches where you can sunbathe, swim, fish, and waterski. You can also make a weekend of it and check out the zoo, maritime museum, Waldameer Park & Water World, and the wineries. Visit *www.visiterie.com* for more information.

Seven Springs

If you're into skiing or other winter activities, there's no doubt you'll head to Seven Springs several times during the colder months. But it's also fun to go when it's warm out—you can take a ride down the alpine slide, check out the foliage in the fall from the chair lift, or bike down the mountain.

(Day Trips, continued)

State College
The home of Penn State University, about two and a half hours from Pittsburgh, is a perfect road-trip destination to catch a fall football game. The drive is beautiful—the hilly terrain is perfect for seeing the gorgeous fall foliage—and it's an experience to watch a game at Beaver Stadium, which seats 107,282.

Weekend Trips from Pittsburgh

Baltimore, Maryland
If you love seafood or history, head to Baltimore, four hours southeast of Pittsburgh. The city is home to beautiful old neighborhoods and some of the freshest crab around. While there, visit the National Aquarium, the Star-Spangled Banner Flag House, the Baltimore Museum of Art, or Oriole Park at Camden Yards.

Cedar Point
Thrill seekers will love Cedar Point amusement park in Sandusky, Ohio, a little more than three hours from Pittsburgh. Called the "Rollercoaster Capital of the World" for a reason, Cedar Point has 17 coasters, including the world's second tallest and the second fastest. The park also has two water parks, a white-sand beach on the shore of Lake Erie, and a children's area.

Cleveland, Ohio
Looking for a weekend away, but don't want to travel too far? Head to Cleveland—it's only about two and half hours from Pittsburgh, and there's a lot to do there. It's home to the Rock & Roll Hall of Fame, which hosts regular concerts, some of which are free. You can also check out the Cleveland Metroparks Zoo & RainForest, the Museum of Natural History, and Lake Erie.

Hershey Park
In central Pennsylvania, about three and a half hours east of Pittsburgh, you'll find a candy lover's dream: Hershey Park. First opened as a park for Hershey Chocolate Company employees, Hershey Park has evolved into a modern-day amusement park with plenty of rollercoasters and rides. But don't miss Hershey's Chocolate World, where you can go on a virtual tour of the chocolate-making process and participate in tastings.

(Weekend Trips, continued)

Niagara Falls

About four hours north of Pittsburgh, you'll find the world-famous Niagara Falls. While the falls are the main attraction here, there are plenty of other activities to fill a weekend. Besides the obligatory ride on the Maid of the Mist, you can also gamble at the casinos (two on the Canadian side and one on the American side), go to the top of Skylon Tower for the highest overhead view of the falls, or shop at the Canada One Factory Outlet.

West Virginia

The West Virginia border is a quick trip from Pittsburgh, but there's enough here to occupy you for a whole weekend. West Virginia has some excellent whitewater rafting, or if you're interested in the state's history, you can take a tour of an exhibition coal mine or meander through some of the small towns. The state is also a major destination for its casinos, including Wheeling Island and the Mountaineer Casino. For more ideas, head to *www.visitwv.com*.

Washington, D.C.

Just about four hours' drive from Pittsburgh, the nation's capital offers a wealth of cultural experiences, including government buildings, national monuments, galleries, museums, and theaters. D.C. is also a destination for live music, international culture and cuisine, and outdoor recreation.

Did You Know?

Top Day Trips from Pittsburgh:

1. Ohiopyle State Park
2. Fallingwater
3. State College/Penn State

Top Weekend Trips from Pittsburgh:

1. Cedar Point
2. Whitewater rafting in West Virginia
3. Hershey Park

About the Authors

Amy Campbell is a Pittsburgh-area native who moved to the city after graduating from Indiana University of Pennsylvania with a bachelor's in journalism. After experiencing city life for a few good years, she finally settled just outside of the eastern city limits, where she and her boyfriend, Jimmy, live with their many cats. They both love everything Pittsburgh and can often be found enjoying a couple of cold ones at Mad Mex or scavenging around Construction Junction for assorted goodies.

Bridget Daley is an alum of Duquesne University. After graduating with a degree in journalism and spending a year working abroad, she fought hard against the prospect of returning to Pittsburgh for no real reason. But like all things good in this world, she decided to follow her heart, which happened to land her in the South Side of the city, and she couldn't be happier. She lives there today with her husband, Chris, and enjoys watching the Pens and winning at foosball.

Matt Hamman grew up in Greensburg, Pa., about 40 minutes outside of Pittsburgh. He moved to the city to attend college at Pitt in 2000 and has lived here ever since, for better or for worse. Though Pittsburgh may be a tough town for a single guy, he loves the city's unique character and hometown pride, and he doesn't plan on leaving anytime soon. If you're lucky, you might catch him in Lawrenceville soaking up the artistic vibes (and maybe a drink or two).

Jen Vella, a Siena College graduate, is a Pittsburgh transplant. She moved to the area from upstate New York about two years ago and immediately fell in love with the city. And even though she gets frustrated with many drivers in the Squirrel Hill tunnels, she can't imagine herself anywhere else. She and her husband, Jeff, just bought their first house and look forward to exploring everything Pittsburgh has to offer, as well as cheering on the Pirates for many years to come!

authors@collegeprowler.com